TRUE FREEDOM

True Freedom

Dr. Verle Bell
with Lela Gilbert

VINE
BOOKS

Servant Publications
Ann Arbor, Michigan

The Scripture verses used in this work are from The New King
James Version copyright © 1979, 1980, 1982, by Thomas
Nelson Inc., Publishers. Used by permission.

Vine Books is an imprint of Servant Publications especially
designed to serve Evangelical Christians.

Published by Servant Publications
P.O. Box 8617
Ann Arbor, Michigan 48107

Cover design by Steve Eames

93 94 95 96 97 10 9 8 7 6 5 4 3 2 1

Printed in the United States of America
ISBN 0-89283-805-1

Library of Congress Cataloging-in-Publication Data

  True Freedom
Verle Bell
      p. cm.
  ISBN 0-89283-805-1
   1. Christian life—Presbyterian authors. I. Title.
BV4501.2.K429 1993
248.4—dc20   93-3610

Contents

Acknowledgments

THE LORD HAS BEEN prompting me to write this book for a long time through the urgings of many friends, patients, and even Christian publishers who benefited from my limited exposition of God's truths.

However, I've seen such awful things happen to men, women, and families who attain some form of recognition, that I wasn't sure I wanted to risk it. Why write the book if no one would read it? And if many read it there'd be the danger. The Lord convinced me he was big enough to protect me from sinful pride in either success or failure and that the ideas weren't mine—just on loan to me to share with his people.

OK, I said, but I asked him to provide a writer to help the truths make the transition from spoken to written words. God took his time, then brought into my life (after I thought I'd looked everywhere) a publisher I'd never heard of and a writer on the other side of the country.

I'd like to thank Lela Gilbert for making these truths come alive on paper. She let them first speak to her so that my thoughts were expressed in a better way. Thanks to Servant Publications for excellent encouragement, editing, and willingness to take a risk. Many thanks to my love, Lois, who supports me past, present, and future as God slowly teaches me my lessons (twenty-two years and five children's worth). As one friend said, "Just how does he know so much about problems and struggles?" Well, I haven't learned it all from working with others, that's for sure. I give thanks to my dear Lord who is so very patient with me and so generous with his abundant love, power, and hope.

1 Infinite, Matchless Grace

THE HORRIBLE SCENE REPLAYED in his mind again and again. The muddy, red road. The little village carved out of the jungle. The old Vietnamese couple walking side by side—directly into the focal point of his rifle sight. Without thought or hesitation, Brian's finger pulled the trigger. As the automatic gunfire cut them down, the old man and woman screamed, fell, and died. Insane laughter echoed in Brian's ears—his own mad reaction to the bloody scene.

Years had passed, and still that laughter mocked him. The impact of those well-aimed bullets had ended not only the old Asian couple's earthly existence but had brought his own life to an abrupt halt as well.

A clean-cut, handsome young man from a Christian home, Brian had been drafted into the army during the Vietnam War. This churchgoing lad seemed to have his life in order, his priorities straight, and his morality well-defined. On the day of his departure for active duty, Brian bid farewell to his many friends from church and school and tearfully embraced his parents and his fiancée.

Soon after the platoon's arrival in Southeast Asia, the simple pleasures of home seemed hopelessly remote. A chilling loneliness haunted Brian. Day after dreary day intensified his emotional yearnings. The letters from home failed to satisfy, never saying everything he wanted to hear. The young soldier's frustration surged every time he received his mail. Why didn't his girlfriend write more about how much she loved him? Didn't his parents miss him enough to write every day? Didn't they care? Had all of his friends faded into the woodwork?

Resentment festered inside Brian. To make matters worse, fear become his constant companion as he watched dozens of mangled casualties being brought back from the front lines. How could he alleviate this inner turmoil? Feeling quite rebellious, Brian began to socialize with some of the rowdier young men in his company. After several weeks had passed, he was partying whenever he got the chance, drinking, doing drugs, and having sex with local Asian prostitutes.

Brian knew he was moving in a dangerous direction. Yet despite his sincere resolutions to stop, this young soldier so far from home couldn't resist the ever-present temptations. Self-control failed him, sending him wildly spinning down a spiral of regret and self-hatred. His repeated failures further fueled his craving for more drugs, alcohol, and sexual excitement.

High on drugs as usual, Brian was taking target practice on the day when his nightmare began in earnest. He bragged to his buddy, "This is no challenge, man. What I need is a moving target!" Kidding around, his friend pointed toward an elderly couple walking quite a distance away. Brian laughed wickedly, aimed his rifle, and shot them both dead.

Once he sobered up and realized what he had done, this young Christian was unable to cope with his guilt and shame. Having literally lost his mental bearings, Brian was admitted to one military psychiatric facility after another for the next several years. His counselors—experts trained to deal with all kinds of battle stress, post-traumatic syndrome, and other war-related conditions—were unable to reach him. They tried to comfort him, reason with him, placate him, all to no avail.

Brian's family and friends continued to pray, even though they had all but given up hope. Then one day he was visited by a doctor he had never seen before. This Christian minced no words "Brian," he said, "When you were in Nam, you betrayed your parents, your fiancée, and all your friends. You abused alcohol and drugs and even committed the sin of murder. There's no other way to look at what happened...."

Brian glared icily at the doctor, hatred flashing in his hazel eyes. Undaunted, the psychiatrist continued, "But Brian, you're a Christian, aren't you? Don't you realize that the atonement of Jesus paid for everything you've done? You are valuable, because Christ has given you value. Your sin is not too great for the atonement of Christ. Is your pride too great to receive it?"

Brian sat stunned by the doctor's words. Even in his mental turmoil, the light of God's truth pierced his darkness. "I'm not too proud to do anything, Doc. You ought to know that by now. So what do you want me to do?"

"Why don't you pray with me? Tell God what you've done wrong. Tell him you're sorry, that you want to start over. Tell God everything. And then receive his grace."

Bowing his head in prayer along with the doctor, Brian received Christ's forgiveness. He was discharged from the hospital four days later with no need for medication or further treatment. Brian had received God's gift of grace and the wholeness that it brings. Psychiatry had diagnosed his condition, but his healing was spiritual.

TOO SIMPLE TO BE TRUE?

Does this young man's story strike you as unlikely or far-fetched? I can assure you that it really happened. Brian's encounter with God's grace occurred just that quickly, and he is still living a healthy, productive life nearly twenty years later. I also know that Brian is not a rare exception. I have been privileged to consult with hundreds of seriously troubled people and have watched similar changes happen again and again.

People often seem surprised by the simple truths that can lead distressed men and women into a new vitality. As you read the following pages, you yourself may be tempted to dismiss my words as merely "pat answers." But having seen these spiritual principles transform the shattered lives of many desperate people, I know they will work for you, no matter what you may be facing.

I've found that people who feel they're handling life well tend to view these life-changing principles as simplistic. It is desperate people who say that they find life and power in them. I've dealt with patients who have suffered abuse in satanic cults, molestation by their fathers, abandonment, the death of a loved one by cancer or suicide, or a traumatic divorce. Those who have emerged victorious will enthusiastically testify to the revolutionary nature of the simple truths contained in this book. Ask God to search you and show you your need so you will be open to see and apply his truth. God blesses desperate people.

God led me into the field of psychiatry through four years of university, four years of medical school, one year of internal medicine residency, and three years of psychiatric training. I then served as a psychiatrist for three years at Wright Patterson Air Force Base in Dayton, Ohio, where I received an Air Force commendation medal for applying God's truth in therapy. I have since worked in state hospitals, community clinics, and private practice. For the past six years I have served in a Christian inpatient clinic.

In the course of my experience, I have observed that both psychologists and religious leaders tend to speak a special language. In doing so, they imply that *growth requires the understanding of complex mysteries* which the average person can't grasp. Although I am both a psychiatrist and a Bible teacher, I prefer to seek the clearest, simplest way to convey truths that work. I have chosen to become a friend with helpful ideas rather than a "professional" who has a corner on some arcane truth that only I can understand.

As a physician and a counselor, I have the privilege of working with people during some of the most painful times of their lives. In the midst of such circumstances, many of them feel worthless, hopeless, and powerless. But if they allow the Lord to come into their lives, he dramatically turns everything around.

Before I explain to you just how God accomplishes these turnarounds, I'd like to tell you a little bit about my personal background as the child of Christian missionary parents. I grew up in India, where we had no television, no stereo, no radios. Life offered few diversions but school, with plenty of extra time to explore the Scriptures. And those sacred words always attracted me. From the very early years of my life, I wanted to serve God in a radical way.

However, I grew up with an erroneous idea about God. I thought that after receiving salvation through Christ, I needed to be perfected through my own efforts. This misunderstanding produced years of struggle and toil. In high school I started debate teams to discuss the Bible. I began a youth group because our church didn't have one. Shy and frightened, I went door to door trying to spread the gospel through personal evangelism. I felt sure all my hard work would please God immensely, or at least keep him from rejecting me. I was saved by grace but, like the Galatians, tried to be perfected by my efforts.

Attending a Christian college allowed me to start prayer meetings and Bible studies. I appeared to be quite a spiritual leader, especially since most of the other students seemed more interested in Ping-Pong than God. But all of this work was done in my own strength. I somehow thought that being so good and doing so much would maintain God's love for me. But underneath it all, I lived in a constant fear that I would fall short.

God, in his mercy, used my very exhaustion to teach me that he already loved me, that I didn't have to earn his love or even maintain it. My next thought was, "Great! Now God can really use me!" But he wasn't quite finished. God still wanted to show me who I was and why he made me that way. Slowly, he taught me to like being myself.

I would like to share with you some of the lessons the Lord taught me during this transformative period of my life. I'm sharing with you as one beggar might share with another: having found the source of food. I'm a sinner who has found forgiveness, a weak person who has found strength. I know that you can do the same. And like the beggar finding food, I must return daily to "feed" on the "living bread."

THE INCOMPARABLE GIFT OF GRACE

People usually look at me strangely when I ask, "What's the most important idea in the universe?" But you'll soon understand why I feel so very strongly about the answer to that question. I believe that the grace of God is the most important idea in the universe.

You see, most people don't clearly understand what grace means. If they come from a Christian background, they sometimes parrot back a definition they've heard in the church: "unmerited favor." But when I ask them what that means, they say "Well, it just means what it says."

Such a high-sounding definition might appeal to our minds but it fails to reach our hearts or our wills. Most of us don't use the word "unmerited" in everyday conversation. "Favor" produces the same blank expressions. The definition of grace as "unmerited favor" is correct but it isn't useful.

Others might define grace as "God's riches at Christ's expense." True enough. Grace is certainly not cheap. Grace had to be free, yet it surely cost God a lot. But that explanation doesn't paint the whole picture either.

Here's a definition of grace that I've found to be extremely helpful.

> Grace is a free, undeserved gift from God to me which provides three basic things to deal with my bent to sin—value, power, and hope.

Don't we all need value, power, and hope? I will expand on their significance to us throughout the rest of this chapter.

If we realistically consider our *past* apart from God's grace, the only proper response is to feel worthless. We've all blown it. In fact, the deeper we probe into our past, the worse it appears. Yet God says, "In spite of all that, I grant you value." He loves us so much that he took the initiative to save us through the death of his Son.

When we look at the *present* apart from God, we realize that we have no power. So God says, "I will be your power." This, too, was purchased by Christ's resurrection and his continued willingness to work in our lives.

When we try to peer into the *future*, we often feel hopeless. But God says, "I have already secured your future, and those who hope in me will not be disappointed."

Growing up in India surrounded by Hinduism, Islam, and various other belief systems enabled me to draw some comparisons. What was the basic difference between Christianity and these other religions? Every religion teaches that it has the "truth," but other religions tell people to be good and to do good in order to earn rewards. I see that as the key difference. Every other religion seems designed for strong people who can earn their way to God.

Christianity is the only religion on earth for weak people. And I'm certainly glad that's the case, because I could never be strong enough to earn God's favor. Thank God for a crutch, I say, for I acknowledge my broken leg. The problem isn't that we're weak and need to be stronger; most of us aren't weak enough in our own eyes to get out of the way and let God be strong through us.

THREE KINDS OF VALUE

According to my definition of grace as outlined on the previous page, God gives us value, power, and hope. I believe that the value comes in three basic types. Oddly enough, each of them can seem to affront our pride. The first is something I call *"just-because value."* You see, we have the same value as a slimy, green rock that a little boy might bring home to his mother. He says, "Mommy, look! Isn't this a great rock?" If you took the rock out and tried to sell it, you couldn't get a penny for it. But if the boy proclaims it to be valuable, then that particular rock is valuable.

We don't particularly like that kind of value. We usually wish our basic worth were more tangibly grounded in our accomplishments, our looks, our social position, our family heritage— whatever. But no, God proclaims that we have ultimate value "just because" we are human beings made in his image.

We receive two other kinds of value totally from God. Because the Creator has done such a good job in making us, we have *"design value."* We read in Psalm 139 that we are "fearfully and wonderfully made."

I believe that God thought you up before the dawn of time

and has been desiring you ever since. He watched over your genetic development through myriad generations. He formed you in your mother's womb. God uses every event from the moment of your birth to add to your unique and valuable design.

But instead of being grateful, we all complain about certain features of our physical appearance or the unchangeable aspects of our lives. And we surely don't approve of some of the circumstances that have left treadmarks on our backs. If only we could begin to see that we are valuable because each of these factors forms part of our brilliant design. Even those harmful actions of others can be transformed to equip us by the grace of God.

We all possess certain strengths and weaknesses. Naturally, we don't like the fact that we have weaknesses; we just want to be strong. Here's how even our limitations make us more valuable. We cannot feel superior to others because of our special abilities, and we cannot be inferior because God says that those who seem the lowest are much more valuable. Besides, if we were good at everything, we wouldn't need one another.

To help you appreciate your personal design value—just the way it is—I would suggest that you create a chart with two columns:

Lord, I thank you that the following things are true:

Column one	*Column two*
Write your God-given strengths and the things that make you useful to others here.	Write your God-given limitations that force you to need other people on this earth.

Besides our limitations, we also bear scars from past sins, our own or those of others. These invisible scars may lead to further wrong behavior, although the scars themselves are not sin in and of themselves. In column two write down whatever personal scars you can identify, thank God for them, and let them serve as constant reminders of your need for his grace.

You can also list your unchangeable features and express your gratitude to God for them. These are neither strengths nor limitations, just facts we often complain about. Try to be grateful for your past, your parents, your brothers and sisters, your spouse, your gender, your height, your appearance, your intelligence, your various physical features, and so forth. It is vital for us to drop any bitterness about who we are, in spite of any pain involved, and be grateful to God for the "design value" he has built into us.

We also have something I call *"tool value."* What do I mean by that? Imagine the world's greatest mechanic trying to make a simple car repair out in the desert without any tools. I happen to be a very absent-minded individual who probably loses about three hundred sixty-five pens a year. A doctor without a pen can have a lot of trouble functioning; he can talk, he can listen, but he can't write anything down. And if an absent-minded doctor doesn't write things down, you can imagine the consequences. Those pens are an important extension of myself, my will. They are valuable tools.

We all need tools. And God chooses to work through people who are willing to say "Lord, you may use my hands; you may use my feet; you may use my mouth." No matter how weak, wishy-washy, or worn out we are, if we make ourselves available to God he will restore us and work through us. Therefore we have "tool value."

Have you ever been involved in a discussion when suddenly God seems to plant an idea in your mind? You can't quite believe grace is true for you or that you are a valuable tool. So to cover yourself you say something like, "Well, this probably doesn't make any sense..." or "This may sound stupid..." or "I'm sure this doesn't apply..." You're not very comfortable speaking out, but you do it anyway.

Afterward, another person comes up to you and says, "I really appreciate what you shared. God used your words to comfort me. It taught me and helped me." And all of a sudden you're confronted with your tool value. God in his mercy took your feeble efforts and used them to help someone else.

Some people become really uncomfortable with this truth. If we admit that we can be used by God to help others, we find ourselves feeling responsible. We can't just go sit in the corner or trash our lives or think about suicide. We begin to realize that we are not "our own" but God's—a needed part of the body of Christ and important to the people around us.

THREE SPECIFIC NEEDS

Pondering the value God has placed in us through his grace, we also come to realize that we are created with three corresponding needs:

- the need to belong
- the need to be unique
- the need to be needed

God wants to fill these important needs. When they are not filled, we experience a terrible emptiness; when they are filled, we find joy and delight. These unfulfilled needs and their accompanying emptiness are not sins and they're not tragedies. They are gifts to us from God. All fulfillment and all pleasure begin with emptiness; without emptiness there is no awareness of need and no capacity to be filled.

Consider the sequence of events in the garden of Eden. God created two of everything and then made only one human being. A little later God said, "This isn't right. It isn't good for man to be alone."

Do you believe God had made a mistake? What was he up to? Why didn't he make Eve right at the same time he made Adam? I think the answer is obvious. Adam began to sense a lack; something was missing. I suppose today we would say he was feeling lonely. Since sin had not yet entered into the picture, Adam's loneliness could not have been wrong in any way. God was simply preparing him for the joy of emptiness filled. When God created Eve, Adam responded with heartfelt gratitude and pleasure. It was a pleasure he could never have experienced if Eve had been there all along. Then Adam would have simply taken her for granted.

God operates in our own lives according to that same principle. He has created our needs in order to meet them.

Let's examine the first need: *the need to belong*. We belong, first of all, to God. But since we are sinners, and God cannot tolerate sin, he certainly couldn't allow us to continue to belong to him without dealing with the contamination of our sin, our need to be made clean. That need has been met because of Christ's sacrifice for sin on the cross. He became our righteousness, our sanctification.

God has provided our "just-because value" through his grace; those who receive this gift by faith have been clothed in the righteousness of Jesus. We can climb into the lap of our "Abba," our heavenly Father as one of his adopted children. We can also enjoy fellowship with other believers as members of God's extended family.

We also *need to be unique*. Hinduism and Buddhism recognize a need to belong. In fact, their ultimate goal is to merge with God like a tiny drop of water merging with the vast ocean. But once that goal is attained, the drop of water cannot be found; it has totally lost its uniqueness.

Not so with Christianity. Our "design value" indicates that each of us is fearfully and wonderfully made. In creating each of us, God has brought forth beings that remain unique and separate and yet can *choose* to belong. When we give ourselves to God, he accepts us but in no way robs us of our identity. He doesn't take away our uniqueness or our freedom of choice. If anything, God gives us more identity than we've ever had before.

God has also given us a *need to be needed*, which corresponds with our "tool value." When we obey God, he chooses to use even our most insignificant efforts. Suppose, for example, you don't know how to pray about something. You go ahead and pray anyhow because the Scriptures say that the Holy Spirit will intercede for you, praying in words and groanings that cannot be uttered. Not only does God take that little effort and make it useful, but he also uses every prayer for his good purposes. Just as we need others to pray for us, they need us to pray for them. Even a glass of cold water given in his name will count for all eternity. And our efforts count even if they don't produce the preferred outcome.

POWER AND HOPE

Besides value, God has also given us the power and hope that we need to deal with our sinful nature. What do people expect when they contemplate the power of God operating in their own lives? Some anticipate tremendous, supernatural energy that will transform them into miracle workers. Others assume that God will do everything for them, that they won't have to exert any personal effort at all. Some speculate that when they bring God's power into a situation, they will immediately be delivered from troubling difficulties.

Karen grew up as part of a satanic cult and had been heavily involved in ritual abuse. This young woman had seen and done things that are almost unspeakable. After receiving God's grace through Christ, Karen had courageously separated herself from the cult but was still faced with a desperate struggle to find her way out of the shameful, horrifying memories of her past.

Because healing seemed like an interminably slow process, Karen described her own perception of God's power in a unique way: "I saw myself in a human cesspool, trying to walk through, with only my nose and mouth above the surface. I cried out to Jesus, and raised my hand toward him. I thought he would reach down, pull me out of the sewage, and lift me into heaven. But instead, Jesus came down, put his arm around me and walked through the filth with me."

The Greek word *paraklete* means "someone who comes alongside." Jesus has personally chosen to assume this powerful role in our lives. He never promised to take us out of the world.

In fact he prayed that we would be in the world, but not of the world (see Jn 17:11-18). Jesus promised to walk through the world with us as our paraklete, our comforter and guide.

I believe the Lord prepares every circumstance of our lives in order to share it with us. He gives us the power to choose his ways and the power to try. Most of all, God provides us with the comfort of his presence and the security of his promises. No matter what trial we face, he will help us through it.

Besides granting value and power, God gives us a hope and a future. The hope we receive from God's grace assures us that he will provide for us tomorrow the same power he is giving us today. He is an unchanging God—the same yesterday, today, and forever. And this hope allows us to perceive as reality what God has promised, even though we cannot see it.

God has committed himself to meeting our need to resist sin in this life and to providing a heavenly home for us in the next. We can fix our hope on those commitments. The Bible says that if we put our hope in God, we will not be disappointed.

Hope is not a feeling but an awareness. It is not an emotion, but an inner certainty. "I know whom I have believed," Paul wrote, "and am persuaded that he is able to keep what I have committed to him until that Day" (2 Tm 1:12). We can know, beyond the shadow of a doubt, that our value, power, and hope are free gifts from God. And we can enjoy the "blessed assurance" that God's grace is, indeed, sufficient in our every weakness.

WORDS AS WEAPONS

Because God has committed himself to us and promised to be sufficient in our every need, it's no wonder that the devil hates God's grace and what it does for us. He knows he can't diminish our grace so he attacks our sense of value, power, and hope. Satan knows that if we feel worthless we're not likely to have confidence or be a very useful weapon in God's hands. So what does he do? He whispers lies in our minds. Every single day of your life you may hear yourself saying things like, "I'm so stupid," "I can't believe I did that," or "What's the matter with me?"

Whenever you find yourself entertaining these kinds of thoughts, be aware that Satan may be surrounding your value with question marks. Every time you're being attacked, take a deep breath and fight back with, "True, I can't earn my value. But I am valuable, just because God loves me, has done a good job designing me, and he works through my efforts. So I will love him, others, and myself."

The devil will attack you on the issue of power, too, because it is the second essential we receive from grace. Every day of your life, you may hear yourself mumbling, "I'm just too weak. I can't, it's way too hard! I give up—there's no point in trying." Or you may be saying, "I've got to try harder. Maybe I can do it!"

Perhaps your objective assessment of the difficulty is correct. Maybe you are facing a huge hurdle. Maybe it even appears to be impossible. If that's the case, here's another weapon to use against the devil's attack. Remember to say,

> I can't be strong,
> but God can help me,
> so let's get started ...

"I can't be strong." Why? Because *I* am powerless. Because I have failed before. Because I am afraid to try again. Because I am unprepared for the task. The list goes on and on. *"But God can help me...."* God is all powerful, all knowing, and everywhere. Most of all, he has promised that I can do all things through him (Phil 4:13).

"So let's get started." The only way the task can be completed is if it's begun. So the sooner we start, the better. Of course, we can assume the devil is going to attack us in the area of hope, because he hates all of grace. The father of lies will without a doubt try to make you feel worthless, helpless, and also hopeless. Whenever Satan assaults your hope, you can quiet your fears by saying, "I cannot secure my future, but God already has, so I will rest in him."

DO WE LIVE IN GRACE OR IN GALATIA?

In order to bring grace into the picture of our everyday lives, we have to recognize when we are forgetting to grab hold of it. We may sing all kinds of beautiful songs about "marvelous, infinite, matchless grace," but most Christians actually hate grace.

You probably say, "Oh, come on. We don't hate it." Unfortunately, I think many believers do. As a matter of fact, I find that the vast majority of Christians don't live in grace at all, but in Galatia. Consider this stern warning Paul issued to these first-century believers:

> "O foolish Galatians! Who has bewitched you that you should not obey the truth before whose eyes Jesus Christ has been clearly portrayed among you as crucified? This only I want to learn from you: Did you receive the Spirit by the works of the law, or by hearing with faith? Are you so foolish? Having begun in the Spirit, are you now being made perfect by the flesh?" Gal 3:1-3

I spent much of my first twenty-seven years in Galatia-territory, saved by grace but trying to be perfected by my own efforts. And that's where a woman named Murial had spent more than fifty years of her Christian life. When this attractive widow came to see me, I could see fatigue in her well-lined face and weary eyes. Talking to her for just a few minutes led me to believe that she was quite depressed.

Nervously tapping her foot and twisting a handkerchief in her hands, Murial described her life, most of which now revolved around an astonishing array of church obligations. And every one of those commitments carried a measure of pressure and personal discomfort. The poor woman was obviously living in works—in Galatia. I tried to probe further. "Murial, I'm used to Christians accepting grace for salvation, then trying to be perfected by their efforts. But you don't even seem to have any memory of grace at all. How did you get saved?"

Murial's face was blank. "I... I've always been saved."

"You mean you grew up in the church?"

"Of course! And I've always been a hard worker in the church. Even as a girl, I worked in the nursery, and..."

I asked again as gently as possible, "But when did you admit you were a sinner without personal worth, power, or hope? When did you ask God the Father to forgive, adopt, and empower you on the basis of the victory of his Son, Jesus?"

After collecting her thoughts for a few moments, Murial admitted that she never really had. She told me that salvation was something she had always hoped to attain by going to church and being good.

I explained that "being saved" is not something that can be acquired by works of any kind, or by the keeping of any law. "True salvation is ours only through faith in God's gift of grace alone, purchased by his Son on the cross."

Does Murial's story suggest any similarities with your own life? Can you recall a time when you paused and acknowledged that you were a sinner, that you were powerless to change, that you were in desperate need of power beyond yourself? Did you ever confess that Jesus Christ was perfect God and perfect man, and that only his death and resurrection could fully pay for your sins and provide hope? Have you ever thrown yourself upon God the Father's mercy, asking him to forgive you, to turn you around, and to adopt you as his child?

If you haven't accepted grace for salvation, I fear that this book isn't going to do you much good. It will probably just make you try harder and burn out faster. After accepting God's free gift of salvation through Jesus Christ, Murial was able to receive grace not only for eternal life, but also for her earthly walk with God. If you haven't yet specifically responded to God's grace for salvation, please stop reading, bow your head, and do so—right now.

OUR STRUGGLE WITH GRACE

Why do Christians struggle so with grace? Because we are human beings. Acknowledging God's grace makes it impossible for us to take credit for what we do. Like Murial, we have to admit that our works will never earn our way into eternal life.

That awareness shines a spotlight on that self-gratifying element called pride.

Another problem arises when we say, "Well, you know, Christ died for everybody, so I don't count." We try to diminish our individual part in that infinite purchase price, thereby cheapening our worth. A key principle from high school math clearly erases that argument. If you divide infinity by the ten billion people that may have lived on this earth, each part remains just as big as the whole. Infinity cannot be reduced by division. Your part in God's infinite grace is still infinite. Feeling worthless can never make you worthless because of the supreme price that has been paid for you.

Grace also threatens our motivation. Apart from grace, we often motivate ourselves by saying, "Boy, if I don't go to church, if I don't do this, if I don't do that, then I won't be worth a thing!" We fear that if we accept our value, power, and hope, we will grow lazy. Maybe we'll even sin so grace can abound—God forbid!

Perhaps a couple of analogies will help to explain this principle more clearly. People who weigh too much fear that they'll gain another fifty pounds if they learn to value themselves in their overweight condition. People who repeatedly give in to bad habits—like drinking too much or frequent angry outbursts—fear that they will get worse and worse if they accept their just-because value.

The reality is totally opposite. When we really accept grace and all that it offers, we gain an invaluable identity... perhaps for the very first time. We receive power to control and motivate ourselves, along with power to influence others. We obtain hope for blessings and direction, for future results and rewards.

Juan Carlos Ortiz, an evangelist from South America, once shared a conversation he'd had with God after having taught grace in seminary for several years. You know how God talks to you and you get these thoughts in your head that are not your own thoughts?

The Lord said, "Juan, why do you teach that stuff?"

"What stuff?" Juan questioned.

"Grace."

"Well, Lord, it's a very important doctrine."

The Lord answered, "Well, I know. It's my idea. But why do you teach that stuff when you don't believe it?"

Juan was shocked. "What do you mean I don't believe it? Of course I do!"

God replied, "No, you don't. All the time you're running around dumping on yourself. If you're late to class, if you don't get your paperwork done, if something doesn't go right, you feel all miserable and put yourself down."

Juan began to see that grace meant that he should lighten up and relax, that he should do his work with excellence but for an altogether different reason: he was already valuable. This new realization gave Juan great peace. But the next morning when he woke up the Lord continued the conversation: "Juan, I've got more to say to you."

"Oh Lord, how could there be any more?"

God suggested, "Well, you know when your wife comes to the breakfast table with curlers in her hair and she's a little grouchy, or when she hasn't done things quite the way you want them done? Well, no matter what, *I* still love her."

Juan responded, "Lord, are you sure you should do that? How will she ever change if you love her that way?"

God said, "Well, Juan, you know, when your secretary doesn't get things typed quite on time…"

Juan Ortiz quickly learned that if *he* accepted grace, he would have to extend it to everyone else as well. And he also understood that he needed to stop using shame and pressure to control other people.

We need to see grace as our divine safety net. "For by grace you have been saved through faith and that not of yourselves; it is the gift of God, not of works, lest anyone should boast" (Eph 2:8-9). Then Scripture goes on to say, "For we are his workmanship, created in Christ Jesus for good works,…"

Let's try to flesh out what Paul meant here. Imagine that one of your friends is learning to work on a trapeze. You go to visit this man and he says, "Come on up and I'll give you a free lesson." You climb up about a hundred feet above the ground and he puts a heavy bar in your hand and says, "Now, just hold on real tight, swing back and forth and I'll catch you."

Before you swing, you notice that the floor is a long, long way down and there isn't any safety net. You say, "Hey, wait a minute! No, way! I'm not going to do this without a net!"

"Oh, you don't want a net!" he says.

"I sure do! Why wouldn't I?"

"Well," he replies, "nets diminish motivation. Now you know it's succeed or die!"

"Thanks a lot! But that's too much motivation. It will cause me to shake and sweat and be less likely to succeed."

Your friend installs a safety net, so you gather all your courage and swing out. Suddenly you slip and fall. No big deal, right? You bounce on the net, get back up, and try again.

Grace becomes a safety net in our lives. Even if we slip, we remember that we still have value, power, and hope. We're not *glad* we slipped, but we try to learn from our mistakes. We don't make excuses; neither do we beat ourselves up.

Grace is not something we just lie down on in laziness and apathy, like a trapeze artist who falls asleep in the net. Rather, God's safety net allows us to learn new lessons, to take risks, to attempt triple back flips from time to time. Grace is always there to help us with those "good works" we've been created to do.

Suppose you do fall off the trapeze? When you blow it, it is not a big surprise to anyone, especially not to God. Our failures are often much less significant than we believe. But when faced with mistakes and sins, we quickly jump to the conclusion that we've lost our value. We feel devoid of power, empty of hope. I believe we place far too much importance on these feelings of doom and gloom.

In fact, by nursing those feelings of worthlessness, helplessness, and hopelessness, we can usurp the authority of Almighty God. We become "the Judge." We say, "God, you have one opinion and I have another opinion and my opinion is superior."

Suppose I asked you, "When you disagree with God, who is correct?" You would say "Don't be silly. God, of course." But in everyday life, we often act like we know more than he does. God proclaims that we are valuable. He assures us that he has placed sufficient power in our lives to do what he calls us to do. God promises us a glorious hope, both for this life and for eternity.

We say, "No, not in my case." We let everyone else come under the spigot of God's grace, but as for us, well, we're just a little too messed up. When we live that way, we're really saying that God's truth is fine for the rest of the world, but it doesn't work in *our* lives. And we hold our own opinion as superior to God's.

From the time my son Robert was born, he was a perfectionist. I think he came out of the womb, looked around the room and said, "Did I do that OK? Boy, this place is a mess. Let's clean it up." He's always wanted to do everything perfectly. When Robert was seven, he took a math test and, horror of horrors, he scored a ninety-six percent instead of one hundred. I heard him in his room, grumbling and chastising himself verbally.

I walked into my son's room, hoping I looked properly upset. I said, "Robert, I don't care what you think. I don't care what your sister says. I don't care, for that matter, what your friends or the neighbors or anyone else says. Whether you got less than one hundred percent on some math test or not, I say you are valuable. And that's the end of the discussion. My opinion is the only one that counts."

Robert was rather stunned, but quite relieved. Being a small child, he was humble enough to accept his father's opinion of him as superior to his own. Even though he felt worthless, his daddy said he was valuable. From that day on, Robert began to learn that it was fine for him to work toward good grades and try to achieve, but never, never, was he to do so in order to become valuable or to maintain my love for him. He was to live and act in the security of my unconditional love.

Perhaps that's fairly easy for a seven-year-old who enjoys the love of his father, but we as adults can be so proud and stubborn at times. It can be very hard for us to admit, "Lord, your opinion is superior to my opinion. When my heart condemns me, you are greater than my heart." May God give us the grace to humble ourselves as a little child.

GRACE IN INFINITE SUPPLY

Some fishermen off the coast in South America were a little careless in their preparations. They had intended to go a short distance down the Amazon delta to fish, but a storm came up and blew them out to sea. They found themselves without a radio, without fuel, and without sufficient water. They floated around helplessly for days in the hot sun, becoming more and more dehydrated.

Finally, just in the nick of time, another boat appeared on the horizon. From a distance these drifting fishermen signaled: "We need water." A signal came back from the other boat, "Just drop a bucket over the side."

The fishermen thought it was some kind of a cruel joke. Everybody knows that if you drink sea water when you are dying of thirst you'll just die faster. They signaled back their objections. "No," came the reply, "it's fresh water. Trust us."

The thirsty men dropped a bucket over the side of the boat and sure enough, the water was fresh. At times, the Amazon's flow extends into the sea for miles beyond the coastline. Dying of thirst, the fishermen had been floating in billions of gallons of fresh water and hadn't even known it.

We are often like those fishermen. We have all this grace around us but we don't tap into it.

Consider another example. Let's say you had a friend who inherited two million dollars but never wrote any checks on the account because it didn't "feel" like he had the money. One day you're riding with him in his old Chevy when it breaks down. He begins to moan and groan. "It's going to cost three or four hundred dollars to fix this car! And to make matters worse, a tow truck charges ninety dollars." Wouldn't you think your friend was a little ridiculous? You'd say, "Look, scrap the thing or give it to me. Then go buy yourself a new luxury car!"

But that's exactly what we do with God's grace. We need to drop the bucket overboard: the water of grace is sweet and refreshing. We need to write the checks: they won't bounce because our grace account is immeasurable. We need to do what Brian, the Vietnam veteran did—he'd lost everything, but he received the grace of God, and his life was restored.

You see, grace is not something we do. I used to think that the biblical instruction to "grow in grace" meant that I was supposed to strive for more grace, to try to gain more grace, thereby turning grace into works. But I was wrong. Grace is infinite and all around us. All we have to do to receive grace is to humble ourselves. To stop trying to gain our own value, power, and hope. To ask God to meet our needs through his grace.

God wants to provide you with everything you could possibly need. I implore you to appropriate into your life all the value, power, and hope that is rightfully yours. It will change the way you live from this moment on. Moving toward true freedom requires an extra measure of God's grace at every turn in the road.

What's holding you back from tossing your empty bucket overboard? I'm going to suggest some possible causes for that kind of paralysis in the next chapter.

<table>
<tr><td>CHAPTER

2</td><td>The Peril
of Pride</td></tr>
</table>

CHAPTER 2 | The Peril of Pride

THE INDIAN COLLEGE STUDENT clutched his hands tensely behind his back as he strolled through the woods near his home. As he soberly pondered his grades, his father, and his future, Raj was surprised to find himself standing in front of a huge, oddly-shaped boulder. He had never seen a rock quite like it in this densely forested area. A strange stirring deep inside made this young man wonder if he should attach any special significance to this unexpected encounter.

Raj studied the rock. Could it be a divine manifestation of some sort? Had he discovered a powerful, unknown diety? He squinted at the boulder. Didn't the indentations in it resemble eyes? He began to imagine a mouth and a nose. Excitement surged within him. Perhaps this new god would provide the power he needed to solve his pressing personal problems. Besides, such a find would bring great prestige in his village. Maybe he would even be looked upon as a guru, a spiritual guide: Raj, the wise.

Inspired and encouraged, the young student rushed back to the family farm, hitched up the oxen and a cart, and headed for the forest. He laboriously loaded the boulder onto the cart and carried it back to the village. He carefully placed this new god under the boughs of an ancient, massive tree.

Word spread quickly. One by one, the villagers brought melted butter and poured it over the idol's curiously shaped form. They placed gifts of fruit and flowers in front of the rock. They whispered rumors about good luck and positive omens. And young Raj, who had brought the god to town, began to feel an altogether new sense of importance. People began to treat this young man with respect. They asked his advice. In the eyes of the villagers, Raj was considered a person of destiny.

Meanwhile, more practical issues pressed the boy for attention. Now in his last year of college, the approach of final exams stirred deep anxiety. Raj's father, a silent, unaffectionate man, had sent his eldest son to university at great financial sacrifice. If Raj failed his exams, he would have squandered the family's money. Not graduating would disgrace Raj before his father, from whom he desperately craved approval. Although he enjoyed the attention of the villagers, no one's opinion meant more to the boy than his father's.

In his fear and despair, Raj floundered around, seeking relief. He even talked to the stone god and pleaded for help, although his prayers sounded hollow and foolish. Deep inside Raj knew the idol was nothing more than an oddly-shaped boulder. In the face of his very real predicament, faith in his stone-faced deity failed him. Meanwhile, nothing quieted the boy's emotions— nothing but liquor. Raj's family disapproved of drinking, and he was ashamed of his own indulgence. But the warm, mind-dulling effects of alcohol soothed Raj's fears, at least temporarily.

Unfortunately, however, the more Raj drank, the less he remembered of his professor's lectures, and the more incomprehensible his assignments became. The dulling of his intellectual acumen drove him to drink more. The adulation of the villagers seemed absurd now. All Raj could think about was the impending exam schedule, and his father's ever-elusive approval.

Even as he labored over the tests, Raj knew he was doing poorly. He couldn't even remember material he'd studied the night before. The student rubbed his face and ran his fingers frantically through his black hair. Panic gripped him on the inside, cutting off what little memory he had left. His troubled mind refused to recall even the simplest facts.

A week later, when the test results were out, Raj learned that he had, indeed, failed his final examinations. He stood dejectedly reading the notice, realizing that he would soon lose the respect of everyone in town who had admired his scholastic endeavors. But far worse than that, the boy would have to tell his father. How could he ever tell his father? Terrible, self-destructive thoughts screamed through his mind.

Raj tried to dull his agony with alcohol, but his dejection only deepened. On his way home from the university later on that day, Raj cast himself in front of a speeding freight train. To the horror of his parents and the villagers, his young life ended violently and tragically. Suicide had seemed to be Raj's only option. What was left to live for?

He had lost all sense of value—knowing that no matter what anyone else thought, his father, whom he idolized, would declare him worthless. Regardless of the brief prestige it had brought to him, the stone god was useless in granting him power. His hope was lost as well, now that alcohol no longer helped him to feel better about his shattered dreams. Without grace from the one true God, Raj's efforts at gaining his own value, power, and hope ended in grim finality.

LUCIFER'S LIE

The grace of God is infinite and priceless, able to give us everything we need. So why is it that we struggle? Why do we fail to keep God's rules, much less to meet our own standards? When we look back at our lives, many of us see a trail of rubble—broken dreams, foolish choices, idolatrous affections, and rebellious sins. And an honest appraisal of our future may not seem all that optimistic. Will tomorrow simply bring a repetition of yesterday's painful patterns?

I have some bad news and some good news for you. The good news is: God's grace is infinite enough to deal with all your sins and failures. Indeed, his strength can be demonstrated through your every weakness. The bad news is: you are worse off than you think.

The bad news can be examined using the tools of basic human psychology, but this approach falls short. I prefer to start with a look at humankind's first encounter with inappropriate behavior. We Christians call it sin.

Lucifer, described in Scripture as one of God's greatest creations, began to rebel against his Creator because of his beauty and glory. He was not foolish enough to think that he was superior to God, but he clearly wanted equality. "I will be like God," the son of the morning said. And thus Lucifer fell, taking a third of the angels with him in this rebellion.

Lucifer, the serpent, then proceeded to entice Adam and Eve with the same possibility: "When you can decide for yourselves what is right and wrong, then ye shall be as gods." They embraced the idea, bringing into the world "original sin," which basically boils down to pride.

What is pride? People would give many different answers: "Pride is thinking you are superior to others." "Pride is thinking about yourself all the time." "Pride is being arrogant." I believe pride can be boiled down to this statement: "I will be my own god. I will try to earn my own value, to be strong, and to secure my own future. I will be the judge of God, myself, and others. By this means, I will create a 'god' which makes me feel valuable, strong, and secure, a god which I can control."

The root of Lucifer's rebellion was trying to usurp God's authority. After many years of closely observing human behavior, I'm convinced that the devil still wants every human being to try to become his or her own god—and thereby come under Satan's dominion. How does he tempt us? By trying to get us to generate for ourselves what we can have only from God—grace. The devil's lie can be boiled down to these three statements:

"I must earn my own value."
"I must generate my own power."
"I must secure my own hope for the future."

I believe that this lie is the root of all sin, as well as the source of much of our insanity. Just as pride robbed Raj of his life, it can rob you of yours.

A prideful approach to life directly affects our will—the part of us that can be governed by basic principles. Let's say you are young and you trust and love somebody. The person betrays or abandons you. You make a decision deep inside that you will never trust anyone again. That's a will decision. Your new principle is "never trust anyone again."

You may eventually begin a relationship with someone who does really care about you. Your mind says, "This is perfect!" Your heart rejoices, "This is wonderful!" But all of a sudden you start doing things that chase the person away. You sabotage the relationship, but don't know why. You do it because you have programmed your will. You have made an unconscious commitment not to get too close, not to trust too much. Your unconscious will, hidden deep inside you, directs your conscious behavior. You tried to ensure your future happiness with a self-protective vow, but it backfired on you.

If we become programmmed to earn our own value, generate our own power, and secure our own future, those intentions will begin to dominate our every action. We decide to embrace Lucifer's lie; we want to become like God.

Let me share with you how the devil typically sets up his little game. If you want to feel valuable, powerful, and secure, all you have to do is be perfect in all areas at all times. Just three rules: (1) I decide for myself what is right. (2) I strive to do this version of right in my own strength. (3) I moan and groan about how hard it is (for extra credit). Pretty simple, isn't it?

Suppose I told you that I would give you a billion dollars if you could be perfect for one day. Would you try? If you thought I had the money, you just might. But, in actual fact, I would be making a pretty safe offer, because I would follow you around and spot some imperfection before five minutes had passed. I would discover either something you did wrong or something you should have done better. To make matters worse, I would probably point out things that you hadn't even noticed.

Many of us live our lives as if we actually could be perfect in all areas forever. We dump on ourselves whenever we fall short. When we do manage to do well in one area, our boosted sense of worth is usually very short lived. Right away the devil suggests, "Yes, you did fine there, but what about this? Look, you didn't do so well in this other area. You're going to try harder."

Pride causes us to feel driven. We become greedy for temporary accomplishments that make us forget, albeit briefly, that we are unable to function perfectly. We yearn for that momentary rush of high self-esteem. That sudden burst of personal power. That fleeting sense of future security. We drink in these transient feelings with great relief, but they never really satisfy us.

A CLOSELY WOVEN GARMENT

Value, power, and hope are all woven together. When we feel a loss of one, the other two seem to be slipping away as well. And when we feel strong in one area, the others tend to follow. Let's take a closer look at what makes us feel valuable, and consider how our sense of power and hope can increase correspondingly.

Value from performance. Most of us attach our value to accomplishments, to our performance of specific tasks. We work hard and then we evaluate how well the task turned out. If we seem to have done a better job than someone else, we feel good about ourselves. If we fail, our sense of value is shaken. We also worry about the future and feel powerless.

As we discussed in the previous chapter, God has already given us our value. Since we cannot earn any of it through any efforts of our own, we commit the sin of pride by attaching our worth to our performance.

Value from possessions. Contemporary Western culture places immense importance on possessions—material things like cars, houses, or clothes. But probe a little deeper and you'll realize that we also "own" (or think we own) many other things like our appearance, our intelligence, our health.

Sometimes we even think that we "own" the people around us and attach our worth to the fact that we belong to an important family or group. While we can attach our worth to all sorts of possessions, our true worth comes from grace through the death and resurrection of Christ. Connecting our worth to our possessions is a slap in God's face.

Value from others' opinions. Personal acceptance and approval are very important to all of us, playing into our very real need to belong. We often attach our value to the approval that we receive from others. When we're rejected, we often feel worthless, powerless, and hopeless. It's fine to belong, but we must not connect our worth to the opinion of another human being.

Let me point out that all of these are fine in themselves. I see nothing intrinsically wrong with doing excellent work, having possessions, or being accepted. What is wrong is relating our worth and our hope and power to these things rather than to the acceptance and approval of Christ.

Value from control. A feeling of being in control also gives us a sense of value. Human nature—with the devil's able assistance—asserts that we must have control over ourselves, our surroundings, and other people if we're going to feel good about ourselves. We may be obsessively neat in our homes. We may be completely preoccupied with "keeping a tight rein" over our finances. We may be rigid in our management of tasks or people we supervise at home or at the office.

We try to control other people in a myriad of ways. We may try to control with guilt, by playing a martyr game. We may use threats of violence or self-destruction. We may attempt to gain control with put-downs, sarcasm, and insults. We also try to control others with the "nice guy" con game, when we try to be so endearing that other people will feel guilty if they don't do things our way.

Unfortunately, if we cannot make people do what we feel is right, we may settle for controlling them in a negative way. If we can't make them like us, we'll make them hate us. If we can't make them feel better, we'll make them miserable. By wielding control of any nature, we believe we have some impact. We'll settle for either positive or negative power, but are often terrified of accepting our powerless condition. We attach our worth to our ability to be in control.

Value from religiosity. One of the most obvious sources of value, particularly among Christians, is religiosity. This approach may involve things like going to church more than anyone else, memorizing more verses, praying more eloquently and appearing to be more righteous. By all means, allow God to take you deeper into worship, into the love of his Word and its application to your practical daily living. But, oh, the deadliness of religiosity!

I've known people who seem to have memorized the entire Bible. They can quote it perfectly and tell you what verse applies to what truth. Yet they habitually lose their tempers, curse, strike their spouses, or fall into sensuality. The Scripture makes no real difference in their lives because they don't learn it for the purpose of meditation and personal application. They simply want to prove how superior they are. Their problems couldn't possibly be their fault because they're such model Christians! I call folks like this "The Forty Pound Bible Club." They often use Scripture to put heavy burdens on other people, but don't attempt to carry those same burdens on their own backs.

Charlotte sat weeping in my office. She was a simplehearted widow who felt her solitude acutely. One of the few comforts of her life was Christian radio. The music stirred her heart and the words of encouragement held out a flickering sense of hope that the future held some promise after all.

But Charlotte had come to see me because she found herself in a terrible dilemma. Because the radio broadcasts often made her feel such a sense of condemnation, she had stopped listening to the radio. In fact, Charlotte was experiencing some rather deep depression. Because of the religiosity communicated over the airwaves by some of these articulate Christian teachers, this woman had the impression that they had no weaknesses or faults themselves. "They are perfect Christians," she whispered to me. "Why can't I be perfect, too?"

As I shared with Charlotte the reality of our ongoing struggle against sin and human weakness, I tried to assure her that I certainly had not arrived (and still haven't!) nor did I know anyone else who had. Even those who admit to problems often express them as past problems now perfected. After she had calmed down, Charlotte said, "You mean you struggle and fight to remember grace and stand in Christ's victory too?" She was so relieved to be able to drop her impossible expectation of being perfect and struggle-free.

These radio preachers probably hadn't intended any harm, but I couldn't help but feel angry at the way their words had discouraged this good Christian woman. Bear in mind how Jesus responded to the Pharisees of his day. The Lord saved his most scathing comments for them, because he could see the pride in their hearts. They were using religion to elevate themselves above others.

My father once told me about a lady who used to attend the church where he ministered. Each Sunday evening Claudia would stand up and say, "I'd like to ask for prayer for my heathen husband, Richard. He doesn't help me with the dishes. He doesn't help take out the garbage. He won't help discipline the kids. Life would be so much better if he got saved."

Then one day, to Claudia's amazement, Richard showed up at a Sunday service and found his way down the center aisle during the altar call. He began praying and walking with God. Before long Richard became a pillar in the church and a dynamic Christian man. Claudia was devastated. She could no longer earn her value by comparing herself with her "heathen" husband. She couldn't draw attention to herself by getting up in Sunday evening service and saying, "Let's pray for poor, lost Richard." It wasn't long before Claudia stopped going to church altogether. She became bitter and rebellious. I suspect this woman was into religiosity, not true Christianity.

BLINDED BY HYPOCRISY

Why can't we see our sinful attempts to earn our own grace? Because we are often blinded by hypocrisy and denial. We try, then we fail, then we say "I haven't failed; I'm not that bad," and then we try again. We run round and round, trapped in our hypocritical efforts to believe the lie that we're anything but the chief of sinners.

We can call this denial. In denial we say, "Yes, I do have to earn my value, generate my power, and secure my future, and I have done so successfully. I'm perfectly fine now!" We maintain a good front. We go to church, preferably teach Sunday school class, sometimes even become a pastor. We work hard, pay our bills, and keep our house in order.

Our commitment to proper appearances can prompt others to look at us and say, "My, isn't that a wonderful person!" However, anybody who knows us more than superficially soon sees that we have imperfections, just like everyone else in the world. But when these weaknesses are pointed out to us, we often shake our heads in bewilderment. "Me? Not me! I don't have a problem."

Be very careful in dealing with people stuck in denial. They will often attack you if you point out any areas of imperfection. They may try to get everyone else in town to attack you. This is especially difficult if you are married to such a person, or have parents who practice denial. You'll feel there must be something wrong with you. Love them but realize all have sinned and fallen short.

One of the most disturbing examples of denial I have ever encountered occurred when a ten-year-old boy named Jason made his way to our hospital one afternoon and asked to be admitted. Earlier in the day, Jason had been sitting alone in his bedroom with the barrel of a handgun pressed against his temple, fingering the trigger, convinced that he should end his life.

Suddenly, in the midst of his desperation, a peculiar thought had come to this young boy: "You're doing exactly what your father wants you to do." Jason had moved the gun slightly, trying to refocus his mind. Again the thought came. "Your father wants you to kill yourself." Slowly, Jason had brought the gun down, holding it with both hands against his trembling body. Tears streamed down his face. Was he just chickening out? Was he a coward? Or was he right?

Jason began to think back over the events of the past few months. His mother had run away with a handsome man from California, tearfully leaving the boy with his father. Jason had overheard his father threatening to kill himself if his son were taken away. His father was a police officer who owned more than a dozen guns, a violent, obscene man who had abused his wife repeatedly. She had always been terrified of him, and would never have found the courage to leave if she hadn't fallen in love with another man. But, tragically, as a result of her adultery, Jason had been left behind.

The father's bitterness had increased as the months passed. He often said to Jason, "Life's really not worth living, is it?" More than once he had remarked, "Someday your mother's going to realize how she's ruined your life. When she sees how hurt you really are, she'll be sorry." Meanwhile, the man was leaving loaded handguns lying all over the house—always placed directly in Jason's path where he couldn't help but see them.

Jason had gradually grown accustomed to the subject of suicide. It had become a familiar topic of conversation. And his father was very understanding whenever Jason spoke about his mother and his feeling of abandonment. "I wouldn't blame you for wanting to blow your brains out, Jason. Think of what she's done to you! Can you imagine a mother leaving her only son?"

In his endless turmoil of grief and abandonment, the boy concluded that self-destruction was the only way out. For weeks he prepared himself to fire that one fatal bullet, and had actually been a split second away from sending it through his brain. Then, at that critical moment, it had occurred to the boy that his father was trying to manipulate Jason into killing himself, as a twisted way of trying to punish his wife. That's when Jason came to us.

After hours of counseling, it became apparent that Jason's intuition was quite correct. But denial reared its ugly head at this point. Jason's father was completely unaware of his repeated efforts to end his son's life. His intentions were entirely subconscious; he didn't at all comprehend what he was doing. Yet this man had clearly set out to accomplish a deadly goal—so clearly that even a ten-year-old child could see it. The human mind possesses the amazing capacity to calculate subconsciously, while completely denying its own intentions.

Fortunately, we were able to work with Jason and his mother. The two of them have since been reunited in California where they are making good progress. The father never became aware of his ruthless objective. His denial was so deep that he could not fathom his own twisted behavior.

Jason's story may be an extreme example, but you might want to take a look at your own responses. If you find yourself repeatedly saying, "No, not me! I don't have that trouble," you may be in a bit of denial yourself. If so, pray for God to open your eyes. And find some spiritual support so that your pattern of denial won't blind you to the truth. Remember our hearts are desperately wicked; only God can search them and show them to us.

We can practice denial in many ways. We may be vague. "I'm sure I must have some problem." We may confess to problems we don't really believe to be wrong. "I'm just too caring." We may claim to be preparing to change, but never actually be doing so. We may constantly compare ourselves to others. "Can you believe how bad he is?"

The Spirit of God is the Spirit of truth. When we use denial as a means of providing ourselves with value, we embrace the devil's lie in two ways. We are playing the part of God in trying to generate our own grace. But to make matters worse, we are also rejecting the Spirit's illumination as he seeks to bring truth to the dark, hidden areas of our lives.

PROVING MY WORTHLESSNESS

Suppose you're determined to generate your own value, power, and hope. You've failed to be perfect. You're not in denial: you know and admit you've got problems. You're tired of trying to be perfect, maybe even burned out. What might your next step be? If you've failed to earn your own worth, you may now try to earn your own worthlessness! You may try to prove to yourself that you are worthless, helpless, and hopeless.

If you know that your value has been purchased by the death and resurrection of Jesus Christ, then no matter how badly you've blown it, you are still of infinite worth. The only way that you can hate yourself and devalue yourself is to reject grace. This rejection makes you the judge. As your own judge, you are repeating the age-old pattern, "I will be like God."

I've seen people work very hard to prove their worthlessness. They say, "Dr. Bell, I've taken every pill in the book. I've been in and out of the hospital. I've seen sixteen counselors, all of them twice as smart as you. And I am a hopeless case."

"Then why did you come to me?" I can't help but ask, "Do you want a certificate of hopelessness to hang on your wall?"

There are no people beyond rescue or repair, beyond the reach of the grace of God. Fortunately, the hope of these desperate men and women does not lie in *my* being more brilliant than those other sixteen professionals. I always ask a simple question: "Do you *want* to allow God to turn you around? If yes, then there is a way out. But if you *want* to be hopeless and worthless, go ahead. Go pretend that you're worthless and hopeless. However, no matter what you do, you'll never be able to prove it because God loves you and give you great worth."

It's amazing how utterly creative people can be in this miserable struggle for worthlessness. I remember one woman who told herself that she should write a book. Then for many years she hated herself for not writing it. Have you ever tried *not* writing a book? It really doesn't take much effort. She felt she was guaranteed to succeed in proving her worthlessness. The way to guarantee that something *won't* happen is to say, "I should." Then you take whatever it is that you "should" be doing, turn it into a club, and beat yourself over the head with it.

We can prove our worthlessness by saying "I shouldn't," and then doing things that we know are wrong. We also can prove our worthlessness by saying "I should," and then *not* doing the things that we know are right.

If you find yourself practicing this kind of behavior, you may be addicted to hating yourself rather than accepting grace. Herein lies a very important truth:

Hating ourselves is just as prideful
as being puffed up and arrogant.

Self-hatred is the rejection of grace. Whether we try to prove our worth or prove ourselves worthless, either way we lose. And in both instances, we end up experiencing pride rather than grace in our lives. This leads inevitably to bitterness and blame, to more denial and escapism.

A root of bitterness can begin to grow when people hurt or offend us. We can respond by pouting, by withdrawing, by not talking to them. When they notice our behavior they usually try to figure out why. We may tell them how we feel they have hurt or offended us. They often become defensive, saying, "Well, yes, maybe I did that, but…" and offering some excuse. Bitterness takes hold when we continue to focus on what they did to hurt us, compounded by the fact that they wouldn't admit what they did was wrong.

Whenever we relate to these particular people, we find ourselves becoming more and more ungrateful for the positive things they do. Little by little, we stop appreciating anything they've ever done for us. Nothing can make up for the wrong they did, and for their failure to apologize. Our bitterness ultimately poisons us. We become bitter at ourselves. We can even feel bitter toward God.

I've seen so many people who say, "Hey, I've dealt with it. I've dealt with the past." Anyone who says that, hasn't! Dealing with the past is always a lifelong process. Instead, these individuals may have watered down the past. They may have said, "Well, my parents did the best they could. It wasn't all that bad." Then they've forgiven the watered-down version of the past rather than forgiving the whole thing. Meanwhile, bitterness can be grinding away below the surface without their awareness of it.

Bitterness must be recognized, because it always destroys us. To illustrate this truth, visualize a little triangle. At the top is the word "God." In the right corner is the word "you" and in the opposite corner, "others."

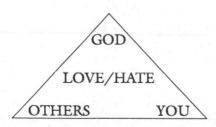

I call this the triangle of love/hate. Think of the person in life that you love the least. That is the measure of your love for the other two. If you hate yourself, then you cannot love God and others. If you hate others, you cannot love God and yourself. The Scriptures say that if you claim that you love God but you hate your brothers or sisters, you lie—the truth isn't in you (1 Jn 4:20). How can you say that you love God whom you haven't seen when you hate your neighbor whom you see every day?

We think it's OK to say, "I love God; I just can't stand people." The fact is, we cannot know how to love God unless we practice on the people in our everyday lives. First we must try to meet their needs, try to reach out and do what is in their best interest. Then we can think about God and say, "I wonder if he feels lonely sometimes when I never talk to him." Just as we've reached out to our friends, we can begin to talk to God—not because we want something, but because we love him and want to share life's events with him.

Furthermore, you cannot say "I love God and everybody else; I just hate myself." The Scriptures say that we should love our neighbor *as ourselves*. I find that if we do not identify our own needs and allow them to be filled by God and others, then we really have no idea what other people's needs are, or how to reach out to them.

Do you put yourself down but pretend that you love God and others? Is there someone in your life against whom you're holding bitterness while you pretend you still love God? Is there any bitterness in your life? It's important for you to find out. Because if you hate any of the three—God, others, or yourself—then you hate them all. It's like a chain: the weakest link determines the strength of the whole chain.

Responding to our supposed worthlessness, we can try to get rid of our misery by placing the blame elsewhere. Blaming others is such a common behavior. "It's not my fault!" we proclaim, refusing to confront our own responsiblity. "My husband is responsible... my parents... my kids... my boss... the IRS... the church... my therapist... our modern culture." The list is probably endless.

We also blame God for our circumstances, for not "making"

us behave, for creating us with weaknesses. "If you'd been through what I've been through you would be this way too," we whine to anyone who will listen. "It's not my fault! Life isn't fair. God doesn't care about me. You just don't understand."

We wallow in the victim role. We may loudly protest our innocence and complain of how we've been hurt. Or we may admit to faults but complain of overly severe consequences. "God is punishing me," we moan. Or we say, "Don't you feel sorry for me? See how I've ruined my life! Poor me!" Then when urged to grieve the losses and let God bring good from them, we protest, "But I'm bad and deserve every bit." When urged to repent and accept God's forgiveness, we quickly retreat and argue, "But I've been hurt so badly."

A third way of feeling better about our supposed worthless condition is to escape into sensuality. What happens when we fail to prove our own worth and also come to hate being our own bitter judge? We may still cling to the desire to create a god of our own, which we can control and which gives us the sensation of being valuable, strong, and secure. Our "next-best god may be sensual escapism. Besides illicit sexual escapades, the most common avenues of escape are alcohol and drugs.

"I would never do that!" we declare in our self-righteousness. It's so easy for us to look down on people who are addicted. Yet any of us can become addicted to something; we just choose to gratify a different appetite. We create a god by consuming a substance or by immersing ourselves in an activity which brings a false sense of relief. This can make us feel strong, valuable, and secure, but the feeling is an illusion. These sensual "gods" invariably control and destroy us.

I believe that we all attempt to drown out our powerlessness in some way or another. I have never met anyone who did not struggle with a sensual addiction of some kind. Sensual means having to do with any of the five senses: sight, taste, sound, smell, and touch. Television, romance novels, soap operas, work, food, recreation, music—lots of activities can drown out the feeling of worthlessness.

Television may lay claim to being the most common addictive element in the world. We measure the power of an addictive action or substance by two things: how easy it is to obtain and how effective it is. Television is legal, relatively inexpensive, starts to work instantly (especially if someone has a remote control), and is very effective.

Even positive activities and substances can become sensual addictions. I have found people who are sensually addicted to God's Word. They can spend so much time reading the Bible that they become essentially useless to everybody around them, including God. We can create our own version of God and indulge in worshiping this twisted picture—God as I want him to be. Some of us create a god by using a person as our source of feeling valuable, strong, and secure. We drain this person dry, seeking constant approval and acceptance.

Even neutral things like fresh water can become an addictive substance. Just try drinking ten gallons of water a day! We sometimes come across patients who have gotten into this sort of pattern. Naturally they feel washed out, unable to go anywhere or do anything because they must constantly visit the bathroom. Water becomes the focus of their lives, with little time left for normal living or facing the facts. They have become addicted to drinking water!

Any kind of substance abuse or other escape into sensuality amounts to creating a god of our own making—a god we can control, a god that gives us the *sensation* of having grace. Addictions help us feel better about our failures. Our little gods keep us from asking God to reveal himself as he truly is. How much better it would be if we simply accepted grace.

FASCINATED WITH SIN

We come into this world having inherited original sin from our parents, which traces all the way back to Adam and Eve. As infants, we remain innocent of the knowledge of what it feels like. Then as we grow, we become curious. God has designed us to be curious, but we make the deadly mistake of being curious about sin—rather than being curious about goodness and God's truth.

We usually don't intend to sin; we just wonder why people do what they do. We may be appalled and disgusted at first, but we feel fascinated, too. We start to examine sin—"only so we can better avoid it and understand it and be appropriately cautious, you understand." We don't realize the grave danger in being merely curious about sin.

Learning all about sin offers no protection. A marvelous poem goes like this:

Sin is a monster of such awful mien.
That to be hated has but to be seen;
But seen too oft, familiar of face
We first endure and then embrace.

At first glance, sin strikes us as disgusting and terrible, but the more we look at it the more we lose our abhorrence for it. Before long, we're asking questions like, "Well, what's so wrong with that?" A part of us begins to think that maybe we just need to taste it a bit to see what is really so bad about it.

Oh, we're not going to get involved, but really, what's the big deal? We feel knowledgeable, even arrogant, in how much we know about sin. Finally the day comes when we actually participate in the sin. For the rest of our lives we will carry the memory of what it felt like. We have aroused the desire to go back and try it again.

But all is not lost. Perhaps you've participated in some kind of wrong behavior and stimulated an appetite to do it again. At this point, you can run to God and say, "There is no excuse. Please forgive me, Lord." If you'll accept his forgiveness, affirm his grace, and lean on his strength not to indulge, after a period of time God will remove the pressure to sin.

But if, instead of repenting, you make excuses, beat yourself, and promise to be strong, you will find yourself slipping and indulging again. And again. After repeating your failures, you will move on to a stage where you are now addicted to the behavior and unable to quit.

Sin can consume us more and more until we become depressed or suicidal. Eventually, we may reach an even more dangerous condition known as reprobation, where we call good bad and bad good. Once we come to that point, our value system has become thoroughly compromised. Perhaps only a major crisis in our lives can serve to turn us around.

Let me illustrate this principle with an allegory. A man trudges home from work. He's tired, he's discouraged with his monthly sales reports and, to make matters worse, his boss has just yelled at him. Grouchy and irritable, he opens the front gate. His children's puppy, which they promised to keep inside, comes running across the yard, jumps up on him, and gets mud all over his pants. The angry man loses control and kicks the puppy halfway across the yard. He feels a surge of relief as his pent-up anger finds expression. The puppy yelps in pain.

The man's spirit says, "That was wrong." He admits to himself that he shouldn't have kicked the puppy, but he rationalizes that he was tired and the kids should have kept him in. He makes some excuses, but promises that he's not going to kick any more puppies. Things go along real well until another difficult day when he comes home tired and the puppy is outside. He kicks the puppy again and experiences relief. He yells at himself, then makes excuses again.

Time goes by and he finds himself walking out of his normal path because he knows where other dogs in the neighborhood are loose when they shouldn't be. When they run toward him, he kicks every one of them. In fact, he buys some sturdy boots so that the dogs can't bite him and he can kick them better. Now he's really hooked. This guy has become an addicted puppy-kicker.

The man tries to get some therapy. He goes to Puppy Kickers Anonymous and admits he's powerless over his problem. But he really isn't desperate. After behaving well for a few weeks and not kicking any puppies, he decides he's doing OK. But sure enough, he soon comes home after a hard day and he's back at it again. He yells at himself, makes excuses, promises to be strong. Pretty soon he gets discouraged over the fact that he just doesn't seem to be able to control his behavior and acknowledges that he's hopeless.

Then the thought begins to come into his head that maybe, just maybe, puppy kicking isn't that bad, after all. It's certainly better than kicking people. Maybe, in fact, puppies are made for that purpose. Maybe God put them on earth so that we could take out our frustrations on them instead of on people. Now the man is headed into reprobation. He even decides that puppy kicking is good. In fact, he organizes a club where members buy lots of puppies and get together every weekend to kick them.

I know it's a terrible example, but I picked a sin we'll probably never run into so that we all can react to it with distaste.

THE MESS OF OUR OWN MAKING

We have seen that first the devil comes to us and suggests that we can be our own god by rejecting grace and trying to generate our own value, power, and hope. And we fall for it, time and again. We think just maybe we can do it. But trying to be perfect eventually leaves us feeling burned out. So we settle for hating ourselves, which allows us to be the judge, but makes us miserable. Then we relieve that misery by trying hard again, by becoming bitter, by blaming God and others, or by burying it all in some kind of sensual addiction, a god of our own making.

Why can't we see our sensual lust patterns more clearly? We fall into a cycle of despair. Looking at our constant failure should make us desperate enough to turn to God, but we usually remain mired in miserable despair instead. We hurt so badly that we just have to find relief. Of course our main relief techniques tend to be sinful habits in which we indulge. "Just one more time; then I'll work on it," we reassure ourselves. Then "one more time" is followed by more despair and around we go again.

Eventually, our downward slide may carry us into feeling suicidal, when we begin to feel that life isn't worth the bother. There are many forms of suicide. We can literally kill ourselves, of course, like Raj. But I find most people don't go quite that far. They just switch off their brains. I know so many people who get up every morning and go through the same exact routine. They go to work, do their boring job, come home, eat, watch television, and go to bed. They may occasionally allow a little variation on weekends, but they never have an original thought. They may have lots of borrowed opinions, loudly voiced, but none of their own. These people have committed mental suicide.

Others bury themselves in sinful behavior and commit moral and spiritual suicide. These people are physically alive but you can't see any sign of real life in their eyes. They are dead in their trespasses and sins. In fact, all sin, all pride, ends in death. "You will not surely die," the serpent promised Eve (Gn 3:4). But, as we know all too well, Satan is a liar and the father of lies.

But don't get depressed! God wants to deliver you out of whatever mess you may find yourself in. I find that God's way out of the pit of guilt is through the bottom. God says, "Hey, you're not just bad, you're worse than you think. Possibly the worst there ever was. So what? Don't forget my grace." In the next chapter, we'll examine the sin cycle more closely in our effort to find the point of exit, the way out to God.

Becoming a Wise Watchman

I T WAS AFTER MIDNIGHT, and the air was heavy with cigarette smoke and the smell of stale coffee. Four officers crowded around the same desk at police headquarters—three local detectives plus an FBI psychiatrist who had been analyzing evidence in search of a serial killer.

Another violent murder had been discovered around noon in a nearby residential district. The four weary men were trying to piece together fragments of evidence, possible leads, and any similarities to other killings. A young woman's sexually-violated body had been found, bizarrely taped and savagely beaten. There could be no coincidence—the same murderer-rapist had left similar evidence in several other cases.

"I can tell you what we have to look for," the FBI specialist began. "This is a white-collar professional. He's normally neat and well-groomed. But by now he's feeling terrible about himself. For the next day or so, he'll stop shaving and be sloppy in his dress. His teeth won't be brushed and he won't have slept. Past experience tells us that this man will beat himself up with guilt for the next forty-eight hours or so."

"How can you be sure?" One of the local detectives narrowed his eyes at the federal officer. "You can't know everything, or you'd have found him by now."

The FBI man yawned, stretched, and nodded. "You're right. We don't know everything, but we know quite a bit. This particular suspect is probably a stockbroker or some sort of financial investor. As far as the rest is concerned, though, it's a pattern with all these guys."

"What do you mean, a pattern?"

"Well, the killer's desire builds up until he attacks his victim and murders her. His craving is satisfied, but he feels repulsed about what he's done—for a while, at least. During that period of regret, he thinks about turning himself in. He may even consider suicide. But before long he's through all the horror and making excuses for himself."

"What excuse could there be for such a brutal crime?" The youngest officer there was still sickened by what he'd seen earlier in the day. "What do you mean 'excuses'?"

"I mean he's blaming his childhood. Or saying his mother ignored him. Or remembering some other woman who hurt him. Who knows? During that stage he's telling himself he'll never do it again. He's going to be strong, and maybe he can get his act together without having to let anyone know about his problem."

"So how long does that last? He's been hitting on somebody every other month."

"My guess is that he'll be back into pornography after a week or two. That's his usual initial compromise. 'I'll just do this, but I won't hurt anybody.' Next thing he knows, the desire to rape and kill is starting to build. He's fantasizing. He's getting excited about doing it again. The pressure grows until he can't stand it any longer. He attacks someone else, and then he's back into remorse again. For the next couple of days, he's unshaved, grubby, and wallowing in guilt."

The chief detective nodded. "The last three hits have been closer together. What do you make of that?"

"This killer is hardening. His regret is weakening, and it's not taking him so long to bounce back. Eventually, he won't feel any guilt at all. Let's just hope we track him down a long time before that happens!"

THE SIN CYCLE

These police officers were discussing a human behavior pattern that takes place all over the world, in every country, in every age group, in every person, and in response to every conceivable form of unhealthy behavior. This pattern strikes a very familiar chord to all addicts, to all abusers, in fact to all sinners. I call it the sin cycle.

In our struggle to remember grace and stand in Christ's victory, we must remember what we have learned about pride and how it manifests itself in our lives. Chapter two presented how pride prompts us to try to be our own god. Creating our own god leads to selfishness, bitterness, and lust. But we are blinded to these realities by the paralyzing cycles of hypocrisy, denial, and despair.

However, we must become more specific as to how we ourselves yield our body members to prideful motivations if we are to affirm the truth and stand our ground. How do we use our minds, eyes, hands, feet, face, voice, etc. to invest in pride? What is our own form of "stinking thinking," "foolish feeling," and "awful actions"? What tools do we use? What are our own danger conditions? We must become aware of our personal tendencies if we are to learn how to be good watchmen. (Warning: We easily assent to the need for self-examination. We know that the Bible teaches that we should make a habit of checking to see if our actions line up with God's will. But many of us are afraid of self-examination. Therefore, we don't do it. We need to admit our resistance, acknowledge that it is truly necessary to our lives, and ask for God's help to become a first class watchman.)

We can identify four parts in the sin cycle:

1. *The Sin:* First comes the actual event—the sinful behavior takes place.
2. *The Relief:* Right after we've sinned, we feel our inner pressure alleviated. We've been tense from trying to be strong up until now, and once we've blown it we've proved to ourselves that we can't be strong. We're relieved to be out of the "I'm-going-to-be-strong" game.

3. *The Reprimands:* Once the tension is alleviated, we launch into yelling at ourselves, saying, "How could I be so stupid? This is terrible! I can't believe I did that!" We try to pay for our sins in some way.

4. *The Excuses:* When we decide that we've beaten ourselves up long enough, we slide into the excuses mode where we say, "Well, what I did was wrong, but I was tired." Or "They made me do it." Or "I've been so abused, and this is just the way I am. I can't help it." We come up with different rationalizations and excuses.

5. *The Resolve:* Once we've excused ourselves, we develop a new resolve. We say that we're not going to commit that sin again and we promise to be strong. And before long, the tension begins to swell within us. It increases unabated until we relieve it by...

6. *The Same Sin—Again.*

What's the way out? Well, as you might have guessed, the answer comes back to grace. When we sin, we have to stop yelling at ourselves. Instead we should say, "What I did was wrong and there is no excuse. Oh God, forgive me." By accepting his forgiveness, we reaffirm the fact that we are still valuable, that the Lord can make something good out of our lives. Most of all, we shouldn't try to be strong in ourselves. Instead, we need to admit that we're weak and cry out to God for his strength.

Every one of us has to watch out for dangerous patterns or cycles of sin. And to avoid getting caught in their perpetual motion, we must cling to the Lord's outstretched hand.

In an effort to better spot the danger we need to become more specific about our sin patterns. Let's begin to examine time cycles that lead to wrong behavior. I believe that we attach a particular sin to the surroundings, the timing, and the circumstances in which we fell. The next time we find ourselves back in those same circumstances, we are likely to sin again. Pretty soon we will have worn a deep groove into our lives, and every time that cycle comes around again, we will repeat that same sin. In between these points we feel very little temptation. It's similar to the eye of a hurricane; we are lulled to believe we are safe. Then the storm of passion hits and we are blown away.

Paul calls this tendency our "old nature." It is the sum total of millions of sin patterns that have been ingrained into our lives. We cannot quit on our own; our grooves are too deep. When God gives us a *new* nature, it needs to displace the old. We need to actively put off the old and put on the new (see Col 3:9-10).

Even though we still have the *desire* to sin, we now have the *power* to run to God, receive help, and overcome temptation. God wants us to lean on him and begin to obey him. And he wants us to do it under the same circumstances in which we used to disobey. In that way, we will start attaching a new meaning to that old cycle.

Eventually, when we continue to obey, our desire for godliness will balance our desire for sin. This time of "hanging in the balance" is a very dangerous interval. People explain that at this point they have little urge to sin. They more typically feel blank, they feel empty, they feel dry. They don't have much sense of who they are. Often, people will run back into the sin because it feels less uncomfortable than their emptiness. However, if we run to God and obey him, no matter how dry or empty we feel, we will soon find ourselves developing a drive toward godliness.

God wants our *wills* even more than our minds and hearts. If we will ourselves to obey because obedience is right—even if our hearts are frightened and our minds resist—then God will undergird our obedience. When the very circumstances that used to drag us down become an occasion for spiritual victory, we will be approaching true freedom. But we may never stand in this freedom unless we learn to spot the pitfalls in the cycles of life.

NATURAL LIFE CYCLES

Cycles help to make life more predictable. Certain occasions come up again and again—yearly, monthly, weekly, or daily. We often attach various behavior patterns to them. Consider the yearly Christmas holidays, for example. We usually rush around trying to stretch our dollars by catching the various sales. Or we buy too many expensive presents, attempting to win everybody's acceptance and affection. We extend our credit and go into debt. In the process we often become harried and irritable and tired and exhausted. Then when Christmas day actually arrives, we feel tremendously relieved because the monumental effort is over for another year. Does any of this sound familiar?

Even though it's my favorite season, I think a lot of sinful behavior has become connected with the holidays surrounding the birth of Christ. People who are struggling with painful memories tell me they hate Christmas. They often find themselves plunging headlong into depression when December rolls around, and repeating the kinds of sins depression triggers. We need to be on guard with respect to these kinds of behavior patterns.

Mother's Day and Father's Day can sometimes stir up hypocrisy or bitterness in our hearts. Rather than dealing with the past and being grateful to God for the parents or children he gave us, we may put on an artificial smile and deny our problems. These long-term relationship difficulties usually manage to resurface anyway, producing wrong thoughts, words, or deeds.

In addition to specific holidays, many seasonal cycles can stimulate the same kinds of patterns. When I was part of a church in Anchorage, Alaska, a curious cycle seemed to envelop the congregation during the summer. The whole work of God would just about shut down because so many of the men rushed out to stand shoulder to shoulder swatting mosquitoes and catching fish! Now nothing's wrong with an occasional fishing expedition, but some of these men went fishing every night, all summer long. They would stay up very late and find themselves too tired to perform well on the job. Their wives and families received little attention. Even though fishing itself isn't evil, the fishermen grieved God by abandoning their primary responsibilities.

We can also find certain behavior patterns surrounding hidden anniversaries. These may have to do with the death of a loved one, a divorce, or a tragedy of some other kind. When that time of year comes around again, we suddenly find ourselves feeling depressed regardless of the current circumstances. Depression is not wrong in itself, but it can often lead to sin. If we find ourselves falling into this kind of cycle, we need to identify *why* we're feeling so bad. We need to grieve our losses, accept God's strength, and receive his promise to work all things together for good for those who believe (Rom 8:28). God's grace can keep us from giving in to sin in the midst of our depression.

Monthly cycles roll around more often. Paying household bills can be an excuse for sin, or even having to balance the checkbook which stubbornly resists all our efforts. Many women struggle with emotional changes related to their female cycle, and have to remember God's grace more diligently during their premenstrual period.

And as for weekly cycles, I've read about the difference between the quality of cars built on Monday and Friday and those assembled in the middle of the week. How many of us moan when Monday rolls around, yet rejoice when it's Friday? It's wrong for us not to do our best job for our bosses each day of the week. And, of course, weekends can be notorious occasions for sinful behavior patterns. We may feel like we've worked hard and somehow deserve to drink too much, to watch too much television, or to overeat.

I often find the greatest failure on the part of Christians to involve Sunday mornings before going to church. After rousing ourselves out of bed a little late, we may fight over the bathroom and begin to feel irritated with one other. Families sometimes squabble and fight all the way to church, then climb out of the car, put on a happy face, and pretend everything is fine. We grieve God by our unkindness at home as well as by our hypocrisy at church.

The daily cycles can wear us down the most. We may rant and rave about that traffic while driving to and from work. Somehow we feel like it's okay to be ill-tempered about so-called neutral things like the weather or the traffic. I don't believe that's the case. Is this a pattern in your life? If so, you may find it helpful to pause when you climb into the car and say, "Lord, this is the time I always have trouble. Thank you for the red lights. Thank you for the rain. Thank you for being in charge of everything."

Take a moment and write down some of the cyclic patterns in your own life, including those which are daily, weekly, monthly, and yearly. Try to remember the trouble spots that come up again and again so that you can seek God's help with them.

OUR INNER DRIVES

In addition to watching for cyclic patterns, we also need to become adept at catching our "self" signals. Certain thoughts, emotions, and actions can warn us of imminent danger. Instead of continuing our headlong rush into sin, as good watchmen we can choose to use these as occasions for falling on our knees and asking for God's grace.

For example, thoughts of bitterness may pop up in our consciousness. "Why me? This is so unfair! How can they do that to me? If they only knew what I've been through..." Or the bitterness may be directed toward ourselves. We may start calling ourselves names, "You idiot! How could you do that?" "You airhead—why don't you use your brain for a change?" "You are so lazy. Get up and get busy!" Somehow we know that we shouldn't call other people names, but we have the notion it's OK to beat up on ourselves. Well, it's not OK. The truth is that you don't belong to yourself; you belong to God. You have no more right to hate yourself than to hate others.

Some thought signals spiral into sensual indulgence. "I've been doing pretty well lately—I deserve a little fling." "What's so wrong with it?" "Just one can't hurt." These thoughts are often referred to as "stinking thinking." And I think that's a good name for them.

"Foolish feelings" can be signals too. People may assume they're on the alert for things like anxiety or depression, and yet miss the early warnings. Why? Because they may be looking for a general feeling rather than specific physical symptoms. How does your body respond to stress or depression? Watch for such things as pressure in your chest, a dry mouth, tightness in the back of your neck, a rumbling and grumbling stomach, and confused, racing thoughts.

I remember one dear lady who called me and said, "Dr. Bell, I haven't been able to get out of bed. I haven't been able to get any housework done. I haven't taken a bath for several days. I'm miserable. What do I do?"

I said, "Well, last time I saw you we decided that next time you got depressed you would use your emergency kit." (I'll explain more about this tool in chapter ten.)

She said, "Oh, but you said that's something I should do if I got depressed."

"Well, what do you think you are now?"

After a long pause on the other end of the line, she asked, "Oh, am I depressed?"

Ruth, a friend of ours, talked to me about her battle with anxiety. I suggested to her that she was playing God by trying to be in control of everything. "No wonder you're tense! It's a big job." We both laughed. Then Ruth forgot about our conversation until several weeks later when her husband was in the hospital with a serious illness. As she drove to see him, she found herself rubbing the back of her neck. It was tight with tension.

"What am I so anxious about?" she asked herself. Ruth began to analyze the thoughts that were racing around in her mind. She was feeling responsible for her husband's health, his future, his comfort, and her own well-being. "There's nothing I can do," she told herself. "It's God's job."

But five minutes later, Ruth was rubbing her neck again. Every time it hurt, the tightness reminded her that she was trying to solve problems that were beyond her power or control. She would relinquish her worries one more time. Before long, Ruth was thanking God for her aching neck. It was a signal to her that she was worrying. It reminded her to release her troubles to the Lord, to leave her life in God's capable hands.

Besides "stinking thinking" and "foolish feelings," certain behaviors or "awful actions" serve as good signals for which we should remain watchful. Consider such things as opening the refrigerator door, withdrawing to your bedroom, squealing the car tires, slamming the door. At first impression, these may sound like fairly innocent activities. But when you're on the lookout for sin patterns such as compulsive overeating, manipulative sulking, breaking traffic laws when you're frustrated, or allowing your temper to rage unchecked, they may not be so harmless after all. If you're a workaholic, your "awful action" might simply be picking up the phone to say, "Sorry, honey. I have to work a couple more hours."

Henry fought an ongoing battle with lust. And his "activity of choice" required him to get into his car and drive to the local X-rated theater, where he could indulge. Now, most of the time when Henry climbed into his car he was going to work, to the grocery store, or to church. But in order to break his particular sensual addiction, he decided that *every* time he got into his car he would pause and ask himself, *"Where am I going and why?"*

To make going to the movies even harder for himself, Henry bought a huge wooden cross and drilled a hole in it. He hung his car keys and a small "emergency kit" on the cross. If he went to a pornographic film, he would have to do one of two things: deliberately remove the keys from the cross or walk into the establishment with a big cross in his hands. Naturally, these measures alone didn't guarantee that Henry wouldn't slip. But along with many other efforts on his part, and a full awareness of his need for God's grace, they helped him turn his life around.

NOTICING WHEN I'M "BLATHERED"

In order to stand in grace, to seek support, to fight back, we must first spot the pool full of sharks, so to speak. Dangerous conditions can arise so slowly as to be imperceptible except to the watchful eye. When we fail to recognize them for what they truly are, they quickly become excuses to sin.

To help you spot these danger times that often lead to sin, let me give you a word: "blathered," the letters of which stand for the dangerous conditions listed below. These are a few of the more common conditions we use to excuse sinful behavior: "Because I'm _____, I can't help but sin." When we find ourselves experiencing any of the following, we need to be cautious and lean on the Lord lest we use these conditions as an excuse to misbehave.

> Bored
> Lonely
> Apathetic
> Tired
> Hungry
> Enraged
> Rejected
> Excited
> Depressed

Boredom can be greatly reduced when we are willing to do our routine duties unto the Lord, to bear our most mundane responsibilities wholeheartedly. If we really do feel we have nothing to do, we always have the option of reaching out to someone in need. Countless men, women, and children could benefit from our love. How many of us have filled our lives with sin because we felt we had the "right" not to be bored?

We often allow *loneliness* to become an excuse for sin. Unmarried or divorced people sometimes feel very isolated. But loneliness offers no excuse for wrongdoing. It was the first emptiness experienced by the human race when Adam was lonely in the garden. Allow your loneliness to drive you to the Lord first, and then take the risks necessary to establish friendships. Don't rush out and fill your loneliness with actions that can cause physical, spiritual, and emotional damage.

The tragic ending of Laurie's story was directly related to her efforts to meet her legitimate needs for love and companionship in her own way. An abused child, this girl married at seventeen to "get out of the house." As is often the case, the man Laurie married was remarkably like her father—an alcoholic abuser. She left him after enduring six months of physical violence.

Within a year Laurie had remarried, and although this spouse was not physically abusive, he was emotionally unavailable. He seldom talked to his wife and wouldn't touch her, except on the rare occasions when he wanted sex. And he refused to work on their marriage. Soon Laurie was divorced again.

In her despair, this demoralized woman began to have promiscuous relationships, one after another. During one year-long period of sexual immorality, Laurie met her third husband. He didn't drink as heavily as her first husband, and he wasn't as aloof as her second, but before long he had found another woman. After a brief marriage Laurie was alone—again.

Through the prayers and efforts of Christian friends, she turned to God and found his grace. His people took her in and gave Laurie the kind of unconditional love she'd never imagined she could have. But her lifelong dream of a lasting, loving relationship with a husband was never to come true. Laurie had AIDS. As she walked through this painful consequence with the Lord, he poured out his grace and fulfilled her dream by giving her a relationship with himself.

God has created emptiness in us because he intends to fill it—in his time, in his way. But when we step in with our own ideas and methods, when we refuse to wait on him, we may sidetrack many of God's earthly blessings indefinitely. God is certainly merciful, yet part of his mercy is allowing serious consequences to happen to us. God will walk through those consequences with us to produce spiritual growth.

As for *apathy*, I can't count the number of times people have said, "Well, Dr. Bell, I've had it with all this. I just don't care anymore. So don't expect me to try." I can understand the feeling, but the fact that we don't care is not an excuse for sin.

What about *tiredness*? "I lost my temper because I was tired." Or "I was tired of trying not to drink, so I stopped off for a beer or two after work." Tiredness does not qualify as an excuse for sin, no matter how tired we get. The same goes for *hunger*. Eat regularly and wisely and you won't be tempted to binge. Furthermore, your moods will be less intemperate if you practice sound nutrition.

Sometimes we become *enraged* and allow our out-of-control anger to explain away words or actions which hurt others around us. Of course we usually minimize our wrongful behavior and call rage merely being upset, hurt, or frustrated. Still all anger not expressed honestly and lovingly masks sin. We must never justify sin. It doesn't matter what anyone has done against us. Even "righteous indignation" at someone else's wrongdoing or evil in general is no excuse for sin on our part. The Bible says that the wrath of human beings does not produce the righteousness of God.

A very dangerous time comes in the wake of personal *rejection*. If someone has rejected you, immediately pause and say, "Oh Lord, help me. This is a time I tend to go out and sin. Help me not to do so."

At the opposite end of the emotional spectrum, we may be very *excited*. When circumstances are going very well we often forget about God and do things we shouldn't. Be especially careful after a spiritually rich time for then we are more prone to temptation. We drop our guard and the enemy comes in like a flood. Likewise, when we are *depressed* we often resort to bad habits to alleviate our suffering.

If I asked you if the devil was a nice guy, you would say, "Certainly not!" But we may be living our lives as if the devil were a gentleman. If you're like me, you sometimes find yourself saying in surprise, "I can't believe it! I never expected the devil to attack me then!"

We should know by now that he always waits until we are exhausted and rejected and depressed. During those low times we don't have our best resources available, we often haven't been praying as much, and we're at our weakest. So Satan takes advantage and attacks. Like a toothless old lion that has to catch the stragglers at the back of the herd, he often succeeds at this kind of spiritual ambush. We need to become more skilled at spotting these ambushes.

Does some hidden part of you say, "Of course I'll serve God, unless..." We often treat God as some sort of insurance policy. "I've done my part, so God must prevent any severe pain or loss or I'll stop doing my part." The devil will ambush you with your "anything buts." Instead seek to be a no-matter-what follower.

As a child I particularly enjoyed a certain musician who sang songs of faith, so I learned them by singing them over and over. Years later I shared at this man's own church how much his music had encouraged me. During my testimony the congregation became nervously quiet. After the service someone filled me in. The man who had sung these songs had done well until his daughter was killed; then he became bitter and drugged out.

This man would have denied that he was a conditional follower of Christ, but his reaction to that severe spiritual ambush had revealed his underlying bargaining mentality. God promises that our obedience will be rewarded by treasure in heaven, benefit to others, fellowship with him, Christlikeness, and ministry to him—but God does not promise comfort or predictability. When caught by surprise we can declare, "Yes, Lord, I belong to you. You are my king and may do with my life as you will."

I could sum up my warning about being "blathered" by this piece of advice: learn to *fear sin, not discomfort or dysfunction.* And when discomfort hits, remember that the fear of the Lord, which is to hate sin, is the beginning of wisdom. Don't fear the discomfort and rush out to escape it. Don't let being blathered become an excuse to sin.

SPOTTING TRIGGERS OF SIN

Besides dangerous cycles, thoughts, feelings, and actions, certain triggers can very easily push us to sin. Psychologists call some of these triggers *transference.* Let me explain by using an example. Have you ever reacted to someone and commented that he or she was *just* like your mother, your father, your brother, your boss—someone toward whom you feel angry? Watch out! When you hear yourself thinking that way, you may be headed for trouble.

A divorce often creates circumstances most ripe for this kind of transference. God has designed children to resemble their parents. For example, the mother looks at her son and he reminds her of her ex-husband. He walks and talks exactly like his father. Actually furious at her ex-husband, she starts screaming, "You're just like your father! I'm going to beat it out of you so you don't become horrible like he is." The boy may in fact be very unlike his father, except in the most superficial ways. This mother overreacts because of transference.

Other sin signals we need to learn how to spot are our defensive styles. We have already talked about denial. There are many other defenses we employ as well. *Projection* is another process by which we defend ourselves. Although we may be hating *ourselves*, we may ignore that fact and say, "No, it's not that I hate myself; it's those people who hate me."

In actual fact, the people we're worried about may not hate us all that much. In fact, they may not think about us at all. But by projecting onto others our own self-hatred, we don't feel quite so bad ourselves.

Another defensive process we might employ is balancing perceived failure in one area by trying to do especially well in other areas. For example, we might say, "Maybe I'm a terrible parent, but I'm a good worker." Or, "Maybe I'm a terrible spouse, but at least I'm memorizing God's Word." This whitewash isn't going to work because God wants us to deal with the problem.

Carly was a medical intern. Her husband, Denny, was also an intern with the same kind of overload. During that difficult year of very hard work, Carly became pregnant and gave birth to their first child, a daughter.

Denny approached fatherhood from a fairly traditional angle. Although they both had the same amount of work to do, Carly was the "official mother." Because of this, she should get up in the middle of the night to change and feed the baby. As the wife, she should also clean the house and do the laundry and all the cooking.

Naturally, Carly was furious at Denny for his failure to support her. But in actual fact, she was even more furious at the baby. Deep inside, she was bitter that this infant had gotten in the way of progress, had made her dream of practicing medicine even more difficult to fulfill.

Carly didn't mind complaining about Denny, but she couldn't admit to herself or anyone else that she was angry at her little one. She often said, "I love having a baby. I just love it!" Every time the child made the slightest noise, Carly rushed over to meet her daughter's needs. But the baby could sense the bitterness and lack of free-flowing love. Although the mother fed her every hour on the hour, the little child wouldn't eat very well and was fussy.

Only when Carly was willing to admit that she was angry at the baby—even though her anger was inappropriate—was this overworked woman able to get help. Facing the facts of the situation eventually turned things around. And Denny discovered that he had a few things to learn about being a loving husband and father.

SPOTTING PERSONALITY IMBALANCES

In addition to common defense systems, each of us possesses a unique personality which we usually begin to express very early in our lives. And within that personal temperament, some of us develop imbalances which are called personality disorders.

As you learn more about how you may have yielded yourself to unhealthy patterns, consider the following common faulty approaches to handling difficulty. You may only have tinges of these or a full-blown disorder. Remember that it's a blessing to see how you're worse than you thought! Specific insight enables you to spot the devil's tactics and to yield yourself to God in new ways.

As young children we may have faced situations which seemed totally overwhelming. We desperately sought some means of handling the stress, and through trial and error eventually found something that brought a little bit of relief. After a while, we may have formed a habit of confronting all situations with the same basic approach.

For us to do well in life we need to be flexible. But if we have a personality disorder, we come at everything the same way. And our behavior "feels" right, not wrong. We may realize that our approach to life isn't working, but we can't understand why.

Let's examine several of the more common personality disorders to see how they can lead us into wrong behavior. Keep in mind that many people avoid these traps altogether, while others may actually combine some of these traits. As you read the following descriptions, ask yourself whether or not any of these personality disorders describe your own response style and to what degree.

One of the ways people deal with stress is called the *histrionic* style. Histrionic children learn that by becoming hysterical, weeping and screaming, other people will come and comfort them. They are rewarded with a certain measure of help and attention, as well as having other people jump in and handle the problem for them. They may carry this behavior into their adult lives, even though they should be doing more and more for themselves. Instead of taking responsibility, those with a histrionic personality disorder easily slide into overly emotional behavior.

As I noted before, this pattern usually develops when young children fail to be loved "just because." They try to get other people to adore them. They cry out emotionally in an effort to gain control, trying to get other people to feed them, provide for them, and solve their problems without having to do anything in return. Later on in life, these individuals will burn out any number of friendships and marriages, because adult relationships aren't supposed to be one-way streets.

Histrionic people are often overly-preoccupied with their physical attractiveness. They loudly embrace casual acquaintances with excessive enthusiasm. They sob uncontrollably over minor mishaps. They unexpectedly fly into a rage. The focus of a histrionic person's emotion is constantly shifting because it is very shallow. Often they seek to be cared for by exchanging sexual favors for "love," thus moving from one relationship to the next with only brief, hysterical remorse.

The *avoidant* personality reacts negatively to all feedback. I remember one person with this disorder who decided she wanted to learn to play tennis. When she went for her first lesson the tennis instructor said, "Well, let me show you. That's not how you hold the racket. Do it this way." He had very gently given her the kind of reasonable instruction for which she was paying. But she couldn't tolerate even that much feedback. This woman threw the racket down and said, "I can't help it! This is my first lesson. Of course I can't do everything right!"

The poor man was bewildered. "Of course you can't. You're just learning. Why are you so upset?" But his new student stormed off the court, never to return. And her problem extended well beyond the tennis court. Every bit of feedback she received caused a similar reaction.

These individuals usually have no intimate friends or confidants. They never let anyone close enough to find fault with them, so they allow only superficial relationships. Even if they marry they remain distant and aloof. Because they cannot listen to criticism, they seldom change or grow.

People with borderline *personality* disorder cannot cope with either failure or success. When these individuals hit bottom they say, "I'm such a failure! I've got to get up and try again." So they'll initiate new relationships, start new school programs, or begin new jobs. Usually quite bright with lots of skill, they quickly find a way to climb out of their pit.

Then as they begin to succeed, they become more and more nervous—terrified of having to sustain the responsibility, afraid someone will resent their success and crush them. They change their minds often about everything. The very people they felt so positive about a month ago soon become their enemies. They abruptly change their opinion about their job, their school, and their friendships. They decide that instead of being full of wonderful opportunities, their lot in life is terrible, just like it's always been. They find themselves sabotaging their success.

What happens sooner or later? These people go crashing back down into the pit where they mutter, "Oh no, I can't stay dependent. I've got to get out of here." So they get back up and start all over again. They are terrified of dependency and failure on the one hand and of success on the other. They have no idea who they are since they derive their identities only from their current activity. When that pursuit collapses, they have to seek a new one.

People with borderline personality disorders will make frantic efforts not to be abandoned in relationships. They may become enraged when individuals they have idealized come crashing down from their pedestals. Both such disillusionment and personal abandonment leave them isolated and rudderless.

People with *depressed* personalities use their gloomy condition as a weapon. Most of the time they seem to be fine, but if someone happens to say what they perceive as "the wrong thing," they'll become depressed, and will direct their depression at the perceived offender. They will punish that person for giving them unwelcome feedback, and soon become immobilized and unresponsive in their misery.

Paranoid **people protect themselves by always being suspicious.** They don't necessarily think the CIA is tapping their phones or that the Mafia is watching them. They just say, in a semi-reasonable way, "You never know who you can trust You've always got to be careful." And so they never trust anyone.

Getting ahead in life requires taking some chances. These individuals are always protecting themselves by never trusting and never taking risks. These people actually expect to be exploited. They are insulted by benign remarks and think people do things simply to annoy them. Consequently they tend to nurse grudges. They won't confront, but will go behind others' backs and counterattack every perceived slight.

Perhaps the most damaging of all the personality disorders is that of the *antisocial*. These men and woman feel that life owes them a free ride, and that they are right to take advantage of others. They tend to be quite clever, able to convince most people that they have no problems and that they are wonderful. And before long they will stab you in the back without feeling the slightest guilt.

People who exhibit antisocial behavior are unable to sustain consistently wholesome behavior. They are often absent from work and are also frequently in trouble with the law. They feel personally indestructible, and believe they can get away with violence, abuse, and unpaid bills. Antisocial individuals often move without leaving a forwarding address. Their problems are always "someone else's fault," and they feel little remorse for their actions. In my opinion, antisocial behavior is the devil's favorite personality disorder.

Let me briefly mention a few other personality patterns.

Passive-Aggressives: those who say yes and mean no. They hide their anger by pretending to be cooperative, and then quietly sabotage your efforts. When you voice your anger, they are ready with an excuse. They will try to fix the blame for their failure on you.

Narcissists: individuals who focus on themselves and feel exaggerated self-esteem. They have a grandiose sense of self-importance; the world revolves around them.

Obsessive-compulsives: people who try to do everything perfectly. They live in a world of lists, laws, and little love. They cannot easily delegate tasks, and they worry incessantly.

Dependents: needy souls who want to please others more than they want to take responsibility for their own thoughts, words, and deeds. They only do what others have told them to do, therefore, no one can be angry with them.

What should you do with this list of personality disorders? We all need to sit down and look at ourselves and say, "Is there one basic way I keep coming at life? Do I need more balance?" As we confront our unhealthy responses to life, we often feel that we're expected to stop being ourselves. Remember that God doesn't expect us to stop being the men and women we are. We need, rather, to gain balance, to surrender our basic pattern to God while seeking the best interests of other people.

We need to be able to come at life from a variety of directions as called for by the situation at hand. There is a proper place for emotion, but we shouldn't manipulate through histrionics.

There is a certain need to be careful, but we shouldn't believe that everyone is untrustworthy. There is value in not becoming arrogant in our success, but we shouldn't be self-destructive in order to avoid it.

Expressing emotion, being careful, and remaining humble are good if expressed in balance, if infused with grace, humility, and God's love. Carried too far and out of balance, even good things become destructive.

TARNISHING GOD'S IMAGE

God created the human race as good, as a reflection of God's image. But our natural urges and life cycles become warped when we try to gain our own value, power, and hope. Because our need is insatiable, greed drives us. We often become angry at God and grow bitter because of our sense of worthlessness. We may become addicted to sensuality in our attempt to drown out bad feelings. We hide from others and blind ourselves to these problems with hypocrisy and denial.

This attempt to usurp God's role warps our wills, changes our minds, and skews our emotions. We need to remain more attentive to the three kinds of "self"-signals which arise out of these sinful patterns of behavior: the things we think, the things we feel, and the things we do. These signals are not so much sinful as they are symptomatic of our deeper rebellion against God.

Whenever these signals—the scars of our having indulged in sin—pop up in our lives, they serve to remind us of our utter weakness and dependence. No matter how well we seem to be doing or how much God seems to be using us, we should never imagine that we can carry on in our own strength. These signals can become especially helpful allies by driving us to God and keeping us close to our only source of value, power, and hope.

In humbly admitting our weakness and our worth, we can energetically identify and spot danger signs in ourselves and in our world. We become able to stand firm, equipped, prepared, and supported. No more being caught by surprise.

My goal is certainly not to make you feel depressed but rather to help you see your desperate need for grace. It is my conviction that until you see that you are among the worst sinners in the world, you won't really feel a need for grace or be filled with gratitude for this wondrous gift.

I would paraphrase Paul's advice to the Romans in this way: "Let's make this real simple because we are human and we are weak. We need to focus on how we've been using the parts of our bodies. Up until now they've been enslaved to iniquity, instruments of uncleanness. Now, consider what the opposite of that would be, and completely yield the parts of your bodies as slaves of righteousness" (Rom 6:19).

We've pondered a bit of the infinity of grace. We've peeked at our need for grace in specific situations. Now it's time to look at the ideal. Where will grace help me to stand? What is the ideal goal? In the next chapter, we're going to discuss the critical concept of humility. Humility before God is the key to emotional, spiritual, and mental health. It is the key that unlocks the door to true freedom.

4 | Humble Thyself

JIM SAT IN MY OFFICE, his head buried in his hands, tears streaming down his burly, tatooed arms. His life was in shambles. Because of his uncontrolled violence, Jim's wife had locked him out of the house and filed a restraining order against him at the county courthouse. He wasn't even allowed to see his kids—kids that he dearly loved. To make matters worse, Jim was being dishonorably discharged from the military for misconduct. Within two or three days, he would have lost family, home, and job.

When I tried to explain to Jim that his life could still glorify God, he stared at me in disbelief. "You've got to be kidding," he muttered. "Not my life! I wouldn't even want anyone to know I'm a Christian. Everyone can see what a mess I am. I'm just dragging God's name through the mud with me."

I again reassured him. "Of course you can glorify God, Jim. The more broken the person, the more God's power can be seen."

Jim was broken, but apparently not quite broken enough. He left my office that day, declaring that he was going to "try again, and try a little harder." Of course that was the last thing he should have done. He was falling into the trap of denial, not admitting how bankrupt he truly was. Jim hypocritically pretended to be able to pick himself up and get back on the right path. I could see by his words and actions that disaster was just waiting to strike.

Determined to get his family back, Jim deliberately violated the restraining order two nights later. He pounded on his front door and yelled, "Alice! Let me in! I want to see my kids! I'm warning you—let me in!"

Alice, who had already suffered a great deal of abuse from her husband, was justifiably terrified. With shaking hands, she dialed the police department. Two officers arrived moments later, handcuffed Jim, and drove him away. That night he at least had a place to stay: the county jail.

During his brief incarceration, Jim realized that he had no options left. Sitting in a drab, depressing jail cell, this man came to understand that trying harder wasn't the answer. He had tried and failed time and again. No longer could he believe in his own strength. No longer could he pretend he could make it on his own. Jim would have to humble himself and receive God's help.

After being released first thing the next morning—which happened to be Sunday—Jim walked out of the jail and straight to a nearby church. He went forward at the end of the service, asked God to forgive his sins, and surrendered his life to the Lord. As the pastor listened to his story, he could see true repentance in Jim's eyes.

Putting Jim in touch with church members provided him with the kind of support he needed to turn his life around. An older couple invited the homeless man to live with them. A deacon offered him a low-paying job, doing manual labor at his store's shipping dock. Jim knew he had to start over, which meant climbing back up out of the gutter. He humbly accepted the offer for lodging and gratefully took the job.

After several weeks of observing his new employee's diligence, the store owner asked Jim if he would be interested in working as a salesperson. Jim agreed and went through the necessary training program. A couple of months later, he was about to be promoted to assistant store manager, when the owner called him into his office.

"Jim, I'm opening a second store and I want you to think about helping me out. How would you feel about managing this store yourself? I'll put somebody else over there to open the new branch." With his higher salary as a store manager, Jim was able to rent a comfortable apartment. By now he had bought himself some clothing, was paying his bills on time, and keeping his commitments at church. Jim had observed the restraining order faithfully, leaving his family strictly alone. But every day he prayed fervently that God would someday allow him to be part of their lives again.

One day Jim's wife called the store unexpectedly. "Would you like to take the kids to the fair tomorrow?" she asked.

"There's nothing I'd rather do." This lonely father fought back the tears that came to his eyes. Was this the turning point?

After a delightful day with his children, Jim was careful to get them back to their mother on time. Hope began to stir in his heart. Were things finally going to change? But for three long weeks afterward the phone was silent. Alice didn't call, and neither did the kids. Jim was beginning to lose heart. How could he prove himself to be a changed man if he wasn't given a chance?

Jim was tempted to give up. To ask someone else out on a date. To go out and have a few drinks, just to make himself feel better. But something in his heart said, "Wait." He remembered a little chorus they sometimes sang at church:

In his time, in his time,
He makes all things beautiful in his time.

Three weeks after taking the children to the fair, Jim finally received the long-awaited call. "Jim, it's Alice. I want to talk to you about something. If... if you're still interested in our family, I just want you to know, I'm willing to try again. Why don't we try going out together, and just see how it goes...."

Because Jim had humbled himself and waited on God, he was about to see God glorified in his life. What kept Jim from seeing the futility of his attempts to be strong? Like many of us, he was blinded by hypocrisy—thinking he wasn't that bad—which led to the delusion that a little more effort would fix his mess and still allow him to take the credit.

HUMILITY OR HUMILIATION?

Why do we fear admitting that in ourselves we are powerless, worthless, and hopeless? Like Jim, we so often keep trying harder to prove ourselves. We stubbornly lean on our own strength. And also like Jim, we may resort to hiding our shame to protect ourselves from the scrutiny of others. We don't want to look bad. Hypocrisy means pretending that we don't really have any greed, bitterness, or sensuality—at least nothing serious that can't be cleaned up by a little hard work.

Sometimes we just minimize our difficulties to ourselves and others. We say, "Well, yes, I do have my problems. But doesn't everybody? Besides, I've been a Christian nearly all my life, and I've pretty much worked through everything. I'm really not doing so badly, compared to a lot of other people I know."

As I've pointed out before, our problems are far worse than we think. In fact, it's only when we recognize God's grace as our much-needed safety net that we can begin to deal with our twisted characters, our manipulative patterns, our self-centered motivations, and our addictions to sinful behavior.

What we actually know about ourselves is like the proverbial "tip of the iceberg." Only about one-ninth of an iceberg actually sticks out of the water; the rest is hidden underneath the surface. Picture that iceberg as your mountain of weaknesses, with the small part sticking out of the sea being partially obscured by fog. As the Holy Spirit begins to blow away some of that fog, you begin to catch a glimpse of just how bad you are. The truth can be overwhelming, which must be why God shows us only a bit of it at a time.

To make matters worse, we can't even see that there is a lot more trouble still obscured by the fog, besides the remaining nine-tenths of the iceberg submerged under the water. The Holy Spirit shines his light upon us and starts to melt some of the visible tip. So then what happens? A little bit more of the iceberg pops out and we say, "Oh no! I really am worse than I thought!"

At that point, it's vital that we reaffirm the truth about our value—that we are infinitely valuable, just because God says so. Once we've become convinced of that reality, God will provide us with the power necessary to deal with our problems. And he has already secured our future, so we have hope—not only in this life but in the life to come.

When we repent of our hypocrisy, accept grace, and admit how much we truly need God's help, we move into humility. Jim did this when he walked into that church. He humbled himself, and in his humility, he received God's grace. Humility is a basic virtue, just as pride is a basic sin. And what is humility? Unfortunately, it is often confused with *humiliation,* which involves dumping on ourselves. And dumping on ourselves is a form of pride, not humility at all.

Humility is liking myself for no earthly reason, but because I have a heavenly reason.

Humility is recognizing that grace is true for me, not just for everyone else.

True humility requires that we see two things at the same time. On the one hand we acknowledge, like Paul, that "in me dwells no good thing." Paul rejoiced, "This is a faithful saying and worthy of all acceptance, that Christ Jesus came into the world to save sinners, of whom I am the chief" (1 Tm 1:15).

Yet, even as he recognized his desperate sin problem, Paul was also fully accepting his calling from God. He verified that he was valuable, useful, and designed to be a tool in God's hands. And then Paul proceeded to turn the world upside down for the Lord. The key to the balance in Paul's life lies in his statement, "... it is no longer I who live, but Christ lives in me" (Gal 2:20).

That's what humility is all about: seeing on the one hand that we have no strength, no value in ourselves, no hope in our future. Apart from God we can do nothing. But if we stop there, we're going to fall into humiliation: "Oh, I'm such a worm." If we get stuck at this low point, we're actually giving in to a perverse kind of pride. We are saying that, in spite of God's grace, my sins are so vast that they overwhelm God's ability to save.

In spite of the fact that we amount to nothing in ourselves, in Christ we have everything. We can begin to act in the truth of his grace, with the understanding that our value, our wisdom, our power, our hope, and all else necessary is available to us because we live in Christ and he lives in us. With such an incredible truth in mind, how can we not be humble?

CAREENING BACK AND FORTH

I think most of us would rather *look good* and be *bad* than be *good* and *look bad*. Let me give you an example. One of my personal heroes is attorney David Gibbs, a man who has richly blessed my life. God also used him in a wonderful way to establish the Christian Law Association. As a young married man with a few kids, it occurred to David that regular church attendance would be a good idea. He reasoned that his kids would become morally sound and might behave better as teenagers. So he started going to church.

Before long, he was asked to be an usher. Being a proper gentleman, he wanted to do his part and became an usher. Then he was asked to be a trustee. "With pleasure," he replied, and served as a trustee.

One day he was sitting in an evangelistic church service minding his own business when God tapped him on the shoulder, so to speak. The Holy Spirit revealed to him that he had never given his life to Jesus Christ. He had never come to the place where he admitted that he was a sinner. David Gibbs was an usher and a deacon, but he was not a true Christian.

The man squirmed a little in the pew, quickly realizing that he was going to have to make a decision. How could he acknowledge his sinful state and throw himself upon the mercy of Christ? How could he receive the grace that had been bought through Christ's death and resurrection? The crux of the problem was that David was embarrassed. How could he walk all the way down to the front of the church at the altar call? What would people think? David Gibbs, a regular member of the church, a leader, a pillar. How awkward to confess that he wasn't even saved.

At that point, being somewhat feisty and stubborn, David said to himself, "Look, I'm not going to go to hell for anybody." With that issue resolved, this pillar of the church got up, walked the full length of the aisle, and gave his life to the Lord.

Could you have humbled yourself in the same sort of circumstances? While God's grace is infinitely immense, our humility is very small. And although young Christians may criticize themselves a lot, they really don't have a good understanding of how messed up they really are. They careen back and forth between pride and humiliation like an out-of-control sports car.

I first learned to drive in India where the roads were full of cows, people, and other modes of transport. I was terrified of killing somebody or hitting a tree or ploughing into the river. At first, the car seemed to have a mind of its own. First it seemed determined to go off the right side of the road. So I'd yank it back, and then it would try to go off the left side of the road. I must have driven up and down our driveway a thousand times, trying to keep that car moving in a straight line.

Even when we get to be good drivers and seem to be able to go in a straight line, what are we actually doing? We're constantly but rather unconsciously making minor adjustments: a little bit to the left, then a little bit to the right, back and forth, meanwhile always keeping our eyes on the road.

Trying to walk in humility involves the same sort of process. When we start to feel bad about ourselves because we've blown it, we need to take a moment to remember who we are *in* Christ. In humility we once again make ourselves available to God. We accept his mercy and cleansing. We ask him to help us try again. When we do, God will bless even our most feeble efforts. Then, when we're doing well and in danger of becoming puffed up with pride, we need to remind ourselves of who we are *without* Christ. We'll eventually learn to keep ourselves on the roadway, rather than veering off wildly in either direction.

When we begin to make progress in learning what humility

really is, we're ready to move on. It's not enough to stop living the same old way. It's time to practice the opposite kinds of thinking and acting. We need to replace our negatives with opposite positives.

Humility is accepting that grace is true for me. This means I believe that I am loved and lovable, empowered and secured. We begin to be enabled to do something—to practice love, faith, and hope. These actions lead to new attitudes which counter the old. Starting with hope, we will examine the Lord's ideal opposites of pride's awful patterns.

Overcoming greed with hope. I define "greed" as our drivenness, our insatiable hunger, our desperate attempts to gain all sorts of things that in the possessing will make us feel valuable, strong, and secure. I believe our greed can be overcome by a new way of thinking. We need to form new goals, new hopes. We need to start reminding ourselves of the following truth:

> I cannot secure my future
> but God already has
> so I can rest in his finished work.

As we implant this thought in our minds, it will begin to work on our will and produce a change. If you recall, our will simply acts based on a principle. We've got a new principle now: we can relax and rest because God has already secured our future. We can begin to act in this new hope, to really plant our feet securely and move ahead in confidence.

FINDING THE RIGHT KIND OF MOTIVATION

What would we do if we truly had hope? We would make plans toward future goals and take action toward meeting those goals. What are your goals in life? Where are you headed? What are you living for? I agree that we are to live in the present. The Lord warned us not to worry about tomorrow's clothes and food, to let the day's own trouble be sufficient for the day (see Mt 6:25-34). But I'm talking about different kinds of goals.

I think we need to ask ourselves, "When I stand before Christ in heaven, what will I have to show for my life?" What I suggest is that we need to change our motivation from the "have to" and the "must" and the "should" and the "got to." These words are tied up with trying to earn our value. Instead, we could say, "It sure would be nice..."

Picture yourself reaching out and helping others, communicating, loving, building relationships. Then picture the rewards that will come in changed lives, in friendships, and in growth. Otherwise we might brace ourselves for trouble, imagining that everything in the future is going to be bleak and terrible. In fact, the opposite is true. Christ has secured our future.

Too often we swing on a pendulum, back and forth between too much motivation (which destroys our performance) and not enough motivation. Let me give you an example of how being *too* motivated can destroy performance.

A confident and qualified physician named Dr. Jackson enjoyed the challenge of working in the emergency room. He was quite accustomed to wild, divergent cases: gunshot wounds, traffic accidents, drug overdoses, critical burns. He kept himself well-versed in the latest treatments and was prepared for anything. Well, almost anything.

One night a call came in that a serious traffic accident had occurred, producing major injuries in those involved. Dr. Jackson immediately alerted his staff, and by the time the ambulances began to roll up to the door, everyone was ready. Dr. Jackson walked briskly over to the first patient and nearly fainted. It was his wife, and she was fighting for her life. In great agitation, he rushed over to the other two accident victims. Just as he feared, it was his son and daughter. His entire family was at risk.

No one could have been more motivated than Dr. Jackson. He had more reason to save those three lives than anyone else on earth. He was well-prepared and powerfully inspired to do his best work. But the poor man couldn't think straight. He ran from one patient to the other, frantic with fear.

Painfully aware of his plight, this doctor did a very wise thing. He called in an associate, and said, I've got to back off, doctor. I can't deal with this particular situation. I'm going to leave it with you." He then excused himself, went into a waiting area, and paced the floor relentlessly while another physician cared for his wife and children.

When their condition had stabilized, Dr. Jackson explained the circumstances to the attending physician. "Thank you for all you've done, doctor. You see, this is my family, and I was just too emotionally involved to deal with their injuries."

If our hope is to earn our grace, to save our own life, then we will be too motivated and, thus, destined to fail. If we say "I'm already secure in my value so it sure would be nice to..." then we find the right balance.

I believe we can ask ourselves seven motivating questions about our purposes in life, seven prayer hopes. I would encourage you to consider these basic questions in regard to each and every activity you undertake:

- How will this bring glory to God?
- How will this benefit others?
- How will this develop the character of Christ in me?
- How will this count in eternity?
- How will this draw me closer to the Lord?
- How will this minister to God by allowing him to work his will?
- How will this affect my inner peace and joy?

How will this bring glory to God? Most Christians have heard that we exist to bring glory to God. When we involve ourselves in various activities, we should ask, "What will people watching me say about God?" Living life for the glory of God is a wonderful privilege.

How will this benefit others? God uses our obedience to bring blessing and benefit to others. The Scriptures say that people need to believe in the Lord, but how are they going to believe if nobody tells them? We not only need to tell people about Christ, we also need to demonstrate his character to them in acts of kindness and service.

How will this develop the character of Christ in me? If we're to be Christlike men and women, we need to choose actions that reflect God's will and ways. We are better able to do this when we familiarize ourselves with Jesus' life, and when we make conscious decisions to follow in his footsteps. We may sometimes find ourselves feeling pain in the midst of our efforts to do right. Jesus will show us that he, too, has been wounded. We are not only sharing in his power, but in his suffering. It is our privilege.

How will this count in eternity? Scripture says we are to be concerned with laying up treasure in heaven. When I was a young Christian, I felt there was something essentially wrong with being motivated by heavenly rewards. But that's not the case. When we begin to think of treasure in heaven and contemplate how we may obtain it, we always feel called on to deeper godliness. Besides, the Lord wants to give us treasure. Wouldn't it be a shame to spoil his pleasure?

I remember one rather cynical person who commented, "Well, big deal. I do all this stuff, I go through all this discomfort, and I get a crown in heaven. So what? The Bible says we have to cast our crowns down in front of the Lord, anyhow."

Wouldn't you want to have something to cast down in front of the Lord? I'd hate to have nothing to give him. Besides if I know the Lord, he'll pick up the crown, polish it, make it a little bigger, add a couple jewels, and then give it back. That's what God always does when we give him something valuable.

How will this draw me closer to the Lord? Oh, to be a friend of the Father! I envy Abraham because was he called a friend of God. But in actual fact, all believers share Abraham's privilege. We have the opportunity to increase our conscious awareness of God, to talk to him, and to draw him into our everyday lives. More than your praise, your service, or your ministry, God wants *you!*

How will this minister to God by allowing him to work his will? I believe that God works through yielded people. When we do not yield ourselves and evil comes in like a flood, it causes God much pain. When we allow God to pour healing through us to others, or even over our own childhood wounds, God himself is ministered to. We also minister to the Lord as we talk to him. What father wouldn't feel pain if his children didn't talk to him?

I think that we have this idea that strength amounts to an inability to feel hurt. Buddhism and Hinduism assert that the ultimate peace, the ultimate joy is to arrive at a place where I don't want anything, I don't feel anything, and I don't care about anything. These tenets suggest that pain is the enemy rather than sin.

We need to recognize that true greatness lies in our ability to be involved, to hurt, to feel the pain of others, but not be destroyed by it. The Lord is that way. If we don't talk to him, he feels lonely. He loves us by entering into our sorrows and offering compassionate and tender mercy. A familiar verse reminds us, "Jesus wept." In the original language, that means "Jesus was wracked with sobs."

Virginia had been my patient for several months when she returned to her family home in the Deep South. She was dreading the trip on one hand, and looking forward to it on the other. For several weeks, memories had been coming back to Virginia's mind—memories about her childhood, her father, and some appalling acts of sexual abuse. Were they true or was her imagination playing tricks on her?

In one particular mental picture that deeply disturbed her, Virginia saw her father overpowering her on his workbench in the basement of their family home. It was such a vague recollection that she wasn't at all sure it had really happened. Nevertheless, Virginia could never manage to forget it. Other glimpses into the past depicted a large, picture window in the living room of the house. And a doorway into the back garden opening from the basement.

This hurting woman wanted to run, to leave her memories vague, to bury the pain. The Lord gently urged her to seek the truth because he longed to bring her healing. He had patiently waited all these years until she had grown enough so that seeing the truth would be helpful rather than overwhelming.

Had things really been the way she remembered them? Determined to solve her personal mysteries, Virginia courageously knocked on the door of the house her family had owned twenty-five years before. A kindly couple in their sixties invited her in. "Of course you can look around. I understand," the man nodded. "Everyone has happy childhood memories, and it's such fun to recapture them."

Virginia smiled stiffly and glanced around. She was relieved to see a small window in the living room. She remarked, "Oh, I thought that was a much larger window...."

"Well, you're right. It was a lot bigger until five years ago. A truck went out of control and crashed into the house. I had a smaller window put in to conserve energy."

Virginia's heart sank a little. Going downstairs, she noticed that there was no door into the backyard. "Wasn't there a door here?" How she hoped he would say no!

"Well, there was. But we never used it. So I just bricked it up a while back. It was right here."

A cold chill rippled down her spine. And what about the workshop? When Virginia walked into the basement, emotion flooded her. She knew immediately, and without question, that her terrible memories were real. But as she approached the workbench where her father had so horribly abused her, she had a spiritual vision in which she saw the Lord sitting there.

With a sorrowful face, Jesus opened his arms to her. Virginia ran to him and felt his tears pour down upon her—streams of tears. Those tears washed away her guilt and the filthiness she felt. She understood that Jesus was not a judge or an impotent bystander but a grieving loved one who had gone through her suffering with her. Somehow, in that supernatural moment, Virginia's healing was powerfully begun. Knowing that her Heavenly Father had wept for her made it a little easier to forgive her earthly father.

Our Lord weeps when we weep and rejoices when we rejoice. His heart is touched by our cries for help and he surely celebrates our joys with us. How God longs to share our lives with us, Friend with friend, Parent with child, the One "Who sticks closer than a brother." Let him work in and through you to will and to do according to his good pleasure (see Phil 2:13).

How will this affect my inner peace and joy? Every time we decide whether we will obey God or follow our sinful nature, we significantly affect our own emotions. Sin may feel good, but the price of sin is pain, shame, and sorrow. We need to count the cost of rebelling against our Maker, both in this life and in the next. Making wise choices today will greatly increase our peace of mind tomorrow.

FREE WILL: GOD'S CHOICE

If we obey God, the rewards are great. However, God will not *make* us obey. I don't know about you, but sometimes I just wish God would make me obey.

As high as the price of pain can be, why does God allow us to make foolish choices in the first place? It's because of his respect for our free will. The Lord often allows great damage to be done to his creatures and his creation. If he prevented all sins, we would have no free will; we would just be zombies or robots.

Perhaps God could preserve free will by allowing some sins, some choice, to happen, while still blocking the big ones—things like incest, or murder, or the beating of children. But who can figure out the difference between big sins and little sins? Do you think you can do it?

For instance, in attempting to serve God, a father may ignore his sons and daughters. He may not beat them; he might even like them and enjoy what little time he spends with them. But this father basically ignores his children because he goes off to "serve the Lord."

What happens? The children feel hurt, feel like they're not worth noticing, feel they just don't count. Ignoring a child doesn't *look* like a big sin, but it can turn out to be more damaging than if the father had kicked the child every day. At least a physically abused child has his existence acknowledged. Many children even spark parental abuse because it hurts less than being ignored.

Bound by his own commitment to free will, God has to watch both our big sins and our little sins being played out before his very eyes. But fortunately God doesn't just wring his hands and give up. He plans ways to bring healing. He seeks agents, individuals to stand in the gap, people who are willing to reach out and bring his love and mercy to bear.

Joni Eareckson Tada is a godly woman who is quadriplegic. It occurred to me the other day that Joni illustrates the way the church functions. Her head works wonderfully well, but many parts of her body just don't cooperate. They want to be fed, nourished, protected, bathed, provided for, but when her head tells them to move they just don't move. Joni's head has to use the few parts of her body that do respond for all kinds of extra duties which they were never originally intended to do. For example, Joni paints with her mouth because her fingers and arms can't cooperate.

The body of Christ functions much the same way. Jesus our head knows exactly what he wants to do, but not all of the members of his body respond to his direction. We often seem to have a mind of our own and a will to do things our own way.

One significant difference exists between Joni's "members" and those of the Christian body, however. Because of spinal injury, her body parts are physically *unable* to work. However, the unresponsive members of the church are usually that way because of their own free will. They have chosen not to take responsibility for the tasks God has assigned to them. Because God respects free will, he allows this situation to continue. But disobedient and unwilling members cripple the whole body.

As one member of the body of Christ, I hope you'll choose to be more than nourished, protected, fed, cleansed, and kept safe. I pray that you'll also become someone who obeys the Head, Christ himself. And when you do, he will surely work through you.

OVERCOMING GREED BY FEAR OF THE LORD

We have seen how God's grace, when accepted, brings us into humility. Humility changes our minds. We no longer feel that we have to secure our future, generate our value, and always be strong. We've learned that we can rest in the Lord instead. And we can begin to further overcome our greed—our drivenness—by doing the opposite of what we would normally do.

So what is the opposite motivation to greed? *Fear of the Lord.* This is a difficult concept, particularly because many people have been hurt by their parents and have learned to fear their earthly father or mother in the wrong way. Our Heavenly Father is not irritable or sinful, vindictive or capricious. It is his mercy that brings discipline into our lives because we need it so desperately. We are his beloved children.

When I ask people "What is the fear of the Lord?" I find that they always get nervous. They say things like, "Well, it's deep reverence." Or "It's respect." I don't think this is enough. I think the word means terror, the kind of terror that causes us to shake in our boots. I believe that fear of the Lord can motivate us to hate evil and to hunger for righteousness.

If you got your foot caught in a railroad track and then suddenly saw a freight train coming around the bend, would you stand still and feel deep reverence? The approaching train is tremendously powerful. You would fear it. Terror would motivate you to struggle free.

God is omnipotent, omniscient, and omnipresent—far exceeding the power of the train in every respect. We choose to obey God in proportion to our awareness of who he really is. We acknowledge the power of the train, and with alarm we realize that we must align our actions with its movement. When we glimpse God's power, we seek to align ourselves with his will. When we grasp how much he loves us, we truly want to obey him.

The fact is, this fear is a form of worship. You either fear God and nobody else, or you fear everybody and everything. The Bible says that the fear of God is the starting place for a journey into wisdom. And it also teaches that the fear of the Lord is to hate all evil. Wisdom itself teaches us to hate evil and to hunger for righteousness. A God-fearing person develops a combination of qualities: an aversion to sin, a desire for virtue, a humble and obedient spirit.

You may ask, "How can I hate sin more? I can't just generate a feeling." True, but you can look at consequences and let God increase your hatred of sin.

One of the assignments we give to people who come in for counseling is to write out fifty ways in which their behavior has damaged other people. After all, how do you learn to hate something? First of all, you have to recognize it and call it by name. Then you have to see its ugly results. That is what we hope will happen with respect to our sinful behavior—enough to motivate us to change.

A judge worked with teenagers who had been arrested for drunken driving. Much to his frustration, he just couldn't seem to make them see the gravity of their crime. These teens had the attitude, "I can drink and drive if I want to. Why shouldn't I? Nothing bad happened. So what's the problem?"

The judge concluded that they were still too young to comprehend the consequences. So he ordered them to spend a few hours in the local hospital's emergency room. Any time victims were admitted subsequent to an accident in which alcohol was involved, the teenagers would have to look closely at the broken, bloodied bodies. They were assigned tasks like pushing gurneys, providing assistance to the health care professionals, and cleaning up the awful mess afterwards. Following that graphic experience, those teenagers had no trouble hating the evil of drunken driving.

Humility allows us to see ourselves as we truly are. We need to realize that we're worse than we thought we were in order to truly hate the evil in our lives. We do this by examining our behavior patterns, our motives, and our past performance. Once we've confronted our evil ways, however, we mustn't wallow in remorse, but move on to repentance, to new ways of living.

THE WAY TO RIGHTEOUSNESS

We can *choose* to hunger and thirst after righteousness. In the Sermon on the Mount (see Mt 5) the Lord says that if you want to be blessed, you should do the following:

- First, admit that you are poor in spirit, penniless, and have nothing to offer to God. Look at your sins without minimizing them.
- Second, mourn over your sins and the sins of the world and realize that things are worse than you thought.
- Third, in meekness stand up to evil calmly in God's power.
- Fourth, hunger and thirst for righteousness.

We can follow these four steps in order to increase our humility and fear of the Lord. Growing in recognition of who God really is will be an ongoing process for the rest of our lives.

In our greed to secure our own lives we had to pretend we weren't "that bad." Learning to fear the Lord sets us free from greed or being driven by earthly desires. With new humility, with new hopes and a new hatred of sin, we can afford to be open and honest. We no longer fear the discomfort that honesty might bring. We hunger for true inner freedom instead.

In humility, we allow the sin to stand uncovered while resting on God's grace for our worth, strength, and security. We confess to God, to ourselves, and to those we trust—who are part of the solution—that we are sinners. We enjoy the freedom of "no more secrets."

5 | Dealing with Bitterness

A S SHE WATCHED THE HANDS of the class-room clock move all too quickly, Susan felt terrified. She grew increasingly preoccupied and worried as the afternoon wore on. It wasn't that she loved school and hated to hear the dismissal bell reverberate through the corridors. In fact, Susan had no friends at school—no one liked her. She wore ill-fitting and shabby clothes, she got low grades, and she never smiled. But compared to Susan's home-life, school seemed like paradise.

Staring out the bus window, the young girl resolutely quieted her fears. Susan reluctantly stepped down onto the street at the bus stop and glanced at her house. As always, her mother's face scowled at her from the window. Soon the woman's voice was snarling at her from the front door. "Get in here! Get busy! You lazy little good-for-nothing! Don't you walk slowly just to get out of working. I know what you're up to!" Then she added injury to insult by swatting her daughter's legs with a belt as the child hurried into the house.

No matter what Susan did, it was always wrong. If she walked slowly, she was avoiding work. If she walked quickly, she was trying to get away from her mother or her father. Her tasks were done under extraordinary pressure. And the tension of anticipating another angry word or the ever-present belt caused the girl to perform even more poorly.

When dinnertime came, Susan was unceremoniously sent to her room as usual. "Her room" was the basement, her bed the bare cement floor. The young child curled up in the darkness while her brother and sisters laughed and ate with their parents. Susan was never allowed to eat with the family: she was too "bad" to sit at the same table with them.

Although quite resigned to her plight, Susan's thoughts often reflected her confusion. "There's something wrong with me. They love the other kids and they aren't mean to them. It's something *I* do wrong. I just don't know what it is." Susan examined herself over and over, but could never find the deep flaw her parents seemed to see so easily. She was a misfit in the home, a pariah, a disgrace. But why?

After everyone else had eaten, Susan was summoned to the kitchen. A bowl of chicken broth awaited her—her customary meal. That particular evening the soup also contained a half a bottle of Tabasco sauce which had been added as a punishment. "You've been a very bad girl today, Susan. And when you're bad, you get your mouth burned."

Tears involuntarily streamed down Susan's face in natural response to the intolerable pepper taste. But her weeping only enraged her mother. "Don't you dare cry! You deserve everything you get! You stop that crying right now and get the kitchen cleaned up. You've still got the laundry and your homework to do!"

As always, Susan had been weighed against the others in the family and found wanting. Of course she was bad. It had to be true. The others never got into trouble. They were not only unpunished, they were consistently well-fed, well-dressed, cuddled, and loved.

Years later, as a deeply troubled adult, Susan came to us for help. I was astonished to learn that, in the course of her childhood, she had never told a soul about her ordeal. No one at school knew. This child had accepted her role as family scapegoat, and in a sense, she had found some importance in it. In her mind she was keeping the others from suffering. And perhaps her assessment was true: her abuse was probably meeting some twisted need in her parents.

As we worked together, Susan began to see that no matter how hard she tried at home, she could never have pleased her mother and father. They didn't *want* her to succeed; they would never have acknowledged her even if she had accomplished something exceptional. Her parents needed someone to blame for their personal problems.

But why had they chosen to blame their eldest daughter? The parents needed to deceive themselves into believing their actions were reasonable. By picking a scapegoat they could tell themselves, "The problem isn't our evil; she's the bad one. See, we don't have any trouble with the others!" Susan felt bitter at herself, at God, and at her parents, but vented her anger in the safest direction. She blamed herself so she could let God and her parents off the hook.

During our counseling sessions, little by little, Susan began to learn that Jesus didn't expect her to be perfect. She didn't have to try to please him. He loved her just as she was. Today this young woman is still making slow but steady progress in her quest for emotional health.

THE WORST OF SINNERS

One of the saddest things in the world is an abused child. Young boys and girls are powerless to alter their circumstances. They are literally trapped, at the mercy of their caretakers. They struggle desperately to find some explanation.

"OK," they may reason to themselves, "I have an idea. The problem is that I'm a bad person, and I deserve all these terrible things that have happened. So, if I am a better person—if I clean my room, study harder, and keep quiet—these awful things won't happen to me."

Invariably, abused children grow up to be adults who are constantly trying to prove that they are valuable by being better and trying harder. Deep inside, they feel unworthy, hopeless, and unable to help themselves. They're locked in a pattern of trying to earn love and acceptance, always unable to love and accept themselves. Such abused people suffer from a deep inner belief in their own worthlessness.

When we come to Christ, we don't come to him saying, "I'm not so bad." We come, rather, by confessing the fact that we are indeed unworthy of his love, powerless to help ourselves, absolutely without hope. We open the door of our hearts not by blaming others or making excuses. We simply choose to confess our condition to the Lord and to receive his grace, by which he promises to meet all of our deepest needs.

A sense of being worthless in ourselves apart from God is very valuable when we're standing on the threshhold of salvation, humbled and in desperate need of God's grace. Empowered by his grace, we need to accept the value which God freely gives to us. No matter what we may have done in the past, no matter what may have been done to us, God still offers us value, power, and hope.

Unfortunately, we often can't receive these gifts with ease. We see the misfortunes that have happened to us and we are bitter. Since the Holy Spirit is now at work inside us, he gently convicts us that the time has come to let go of our bitterness. We want to comply. But it's not as easy as it sounds. Forgiveness often looks like the widest chasm we've ever seen.

How do we purge ourselves of the poison of bitterness and forgive those who have hurt us? Bitterness boils down to hating ourselves because of our failures, hating God for what he has allowed into our lives, and hating others for their part in it all. In humility, we need to pause and say "I am the chief of sinners. I need help."

As the worst of sinners, we can no longer see ourselves as innocent victims. We can no longer feel righteously consumed with anger and bitterness toward those who have caused us pain. In our worst moments, we are fully capable of being just as destructive. In fact, truth be known, we've probably done worse things than they have.

Once we've accepted that fact, we need to move beyond it, which means getting our minds turned around. Why do we feel bitter? Because we feel that we have no value. At the core of our being, we feel like worthless failures. When you are beating up on yourself, pause for a moment and repeat this truth:

I can't generate my value.
But no matter what, I am valuable—just because.
God has done a good job on me.
And if I try, God will bless my feeble efforts.

When we realize what God has done for us and begin to feel valuable in his sight, we're able to accept his forgiveness despite all the problems of the past. This releases us from bitterness against ourselves. We confess, "Yes, I am a sinner, but I'm redeemed by the grace of God. Now perhaps I can reach out to others."

FACE THE PAST AT ITS WORST

We all struggle with bitterness at some point in our walk with Christ. When we look over our past, we can find it hard to accept the full load of the pain and problems we've suffered. Sometimes we try to water it all down. Minimizing past hurts makes them easier for us to forgive. Diminishing the severity of abuses allows us to more readily live with the resulting damage. After extending a partial forgiveness to those who may have hurt us, we think that we'll finally be able to move ahead in freedom.

But not confronting the past at face value also makes our forgiveness rather meaningless. Even if the mind has forgotten the worst details, the heart knows what really happened.

So many people come to me and say about their pain, "I've worked through it." What they have dealt with is the watered-down version. A classic statement is frequently made about parents: "They did the best they could." While it sounds generous, it is in fact irrational from my standpoint. The best that any one of us can do by ourselves will ultimately ruin our children. Only when we go to God and allow him to work through us can we entertain any hope of doing a good job in our parenting. If your parents really did the best *they* could, without God, then that means they have let you down badly.

Those who have hurt us have done so while exercising their free will. They could have gone to God for grace and guidance. They may have decided not to. When we say, "They did their best," we're trying to let people who are important to us—our parents, our teachers, our siblings, or whomever—off the hook. That way we don't have to face up to the real circumstances, truly grieve over them, and thoroughly forgive.

We walk a fine line here. Just as it is important to face the full impact of our personal history, it is equally important that we not get stuck wallowing in the details of past evil. Even after we've gone through the grieving and forgiving process, devastating details will sometimes come back to haunt us. Something may trigger a memory—a father's face, a mother's tone of voice, a husband's indifference, a wife's criticism, a trip to our hometown, a song, a photograph, a holiday. The devil will stir up the past at just the right time to try to keep us from moving forward with God.

Bob was a hard-working man, ambitious and greedy for success. His obsession with his career left him little time for his attractive wife Abigail. Lonely and bored, she sat at home alone nearly every night of the week. She prepared countless scrumptious dinners for her husband, lit the candles, and turned on soft music—only to hear the phone ring half an hour after his expected arrival time.

"Sorry, love, I won't be home for dinner. I've got to get this proposal together by tomorrow morning." The gourmet feast sat cold and uneaten on the stove while Bob labored at the office into the wee hours of the morning.

While Bob and Abigail made sure to attend church, this husband failed to provide Christian leadership in their home. Abigail's spiritual emptiness, along with her solitude, made her a prime candidate for an extramarital affair. And it wasn't long before she had one.

Adultery is clearly wrong. This woman could have gone to God for the grace not to get involved with another man. Abigail could have confronted her husband and insisted that they work on the marriage. If she had, God could have helped Bob examine himself and realize his serious weaknesses. With God's help, he could have changed.

But unfortunately things don't always work the way they should. A torrid affair raged for months. And to make matters worse, Bob came across some love letters this man had written to his wife. These weren't just ordinary love letters, either. They contained sexually explicit, lustful particulars about their relationship.

Bob's head was full of all these sordid details as he pondered how he should approach his wife. Sometimes the Holy Spirit would nudge him and say, "What about you? Are you dealing with your sins and your shortcomings? You're the one who was supposed to be the spiritual leader. You're the one who will have to give account to God for the part you played in your wife's affair."

His heart hardened with bitterness, Bob was unable to receive the Spirit's gentle counsel. He would sputter, "But, but, but…" and then start to review the lurid details of the affair. Instead of repentance, Bob was overcome with rage. On one occasion he become so incensed that he knocked Abigail down and left her lying half-conscious on the floor, only to walk over to the church less than an hour later to share his testimony with a men's group. And still he seemed unable to recognize his own hypocrisy.

It is amazing what we can do if we get stuck in the details of evil. We can often justify any amount of personal sin. By refusing to grieve and repent, Bob slowly sank into insanity. Tragically, he still resides in a state hospital today.

REMEMBERING—GOD'S WAY

In Bob's case, nothing was hidden about his wife's affair. The actions he needed to mourn and forgive, unwelcome as they were, had been clearly laid out for him. But so often—particularly with regards to childhood circumstances—our minds have blanked out episodes and events that may be extremely significant. We find ourselves damaged by past circumstances—the evidence of abuse is clearly there—but we cannot recall what, when, or how the damage was done.

How do we remember what our minds refuse to recall? Entire blocks of memory may be completely lost. Human beings have a great capacity to deny painful experiences to such a degree that they can't recollect them at all. If you suspect that there are some forgotten occurrences that lie buried within your own life, I advise you to copy the following prayer on a piece of paper.

Lord, I give you permission to show me details from the past that I need to see—whatever I am able to recall without becoming more bitter. I also give you permission to hide from me details from the past which I am not yet ready to see.

The Lord must be sovereign over every aspect of our efforts to remember the past if we are to benefit. Psychiatrists have all kinds of techniques that can help people get in touch with past memories. But if patients are not ready to grasp God's truths, they may be destroyed by those memories.

I remember one lady who informed me, "I've got to get in touch with the past. I've got to deal with it. I've got to get over it! I've got to move forward, and if you don't hypnotize me or give me sodium amytal, I'll go find someone who will."

I shook my head rather sadly and then responded. "Well, I'm sorry you're choosing to do things that way. I think that God would work with you here without those artificial means. If you go ahead with your plan, you certainly will remember the past. And you'll wish you hadn't. You will be full of bitterness at God, at yourself, and at everybody else involved."

The woman backed off and agreed to write out the commitment which I suggested above, stating that God could choose when and what she remembered. Meanwhile, she poured herself into answering these sorts of questions:

- How can a loving God allow bad things to happen?
- How does God take damage and turn it into new growth?

- How does God bring good out of evil?
- How does God pour out his grace?
- How can I cooperate with God?

In the weeks that followed this woman remembered a lot more than she wanted to. But the tragic details of her past did not destroy her because she had submitted herself to God's care. She had decided to allow the Master Healer to determine what she should remember and what she shouldn't.

I have seen enormous damage result when people are forced to remember memories for which they are unprepared. And damage is also done when they are forced to focus on every gory detail of their past before getting on with life. The process of healing and growth lasts all our lives. The Lord may not even choose to uncover certain memories for reasons of his own. Let God be sovereign over your remembering. Focus on obedience and responsibility in the present, no matter what does or doesn't surface.

Another patient of ours wasn't so sure she wanted to believe that her memories were accurate. She vacillated between thinking that certain things had really happened between her and her father, and concluding that she had an overactive imagination. We assured her that we believed her memories were consistent and represented actual events. But she left therapy in order to continue her denial.

Finally this woman grew weary of her pain but decided to be admitted to a different hospital. Their counselors asserted that she most certainly had imagined those incestuous incidents. "Yes, your memories are fabrications. Yes, we're convinced that you've dreamed up those encounters. No, you're not the victim of sexual abuse."

Somehow, this unyielding position actually served to bring this woman to terms with the truth of her past. Once she tried to forthrightly deny the existence of these painful incidents, she realized that there was no possible way she could. The memories were undeniably real; they were unquestionably true.

This woman came to see that her task was not to *eliminate* the memories, but to work through them, along with the excruciating emotions they evoked. Her goal was not supposed to be denial, but accepting and living in reality, forgiving those who had wounded her and receiving healing through the grace of God.

COMING OUT OF THE FOG

As you begin to submit to God's process, you may find yourself confronted with rather foggy memories of the past. Slowly the memories will start emerging and the fog of denial will begin to thin. Usually, like the woman I just mentioned, people think, "Boy, what an imagination I've got! Maybe I've been reading too many books or watching too many movies. I'm sure that couldn't have happened." Gradually the details become more and more clear. Let me detail the various stages through which you may pass in clarifying your memory.

Becoming a reporter. From the fog of denial, we often move into the reporter stage. Have you ever listened to the news? Reporters seem to be able to cover the most hideous incidents with firm, professional tones or no vocal expression at all. Seconds later, they move on to sports or weather and instantly become cheerful and chipper—while I'm still emotionally reeling from the tragedy they reported moments earlier. "Hey, wait a minute." I ask myself. "Can't you at least show a little sorrow over the pain and misery of others?"

I call it the "reporter stage" when people can reveal horrible things from the past almost as if they were entertained by them or as if these incidents had happened to a total stranger. I've had patients tell me unbelievably disgusting stories with complete detachment. Of course this is a protective device. If you're in that stage, don't be mad at yourself. Don't say, "What's the matter with me? Why can't I cry? Why can't I feel?" Instead, thank God that he has given you the memories before giving you the feelings which may only devastate you.

Feeling your feelings. As you make progress in probing your past, you will move beyond the reporter stage into the feeling stage. Three basic feelings typically flood in and out, back and forth like the ocean tide.

First we feel *rage and anger*, sometimes directed at God. "Why did he let this happen? He should have stopped it!" We may berate ourselves for being weak and allowing it to happen, or perhaps even blame ourselves for *causing* it to happen.

Second comes a feeling of *sorrow*. We experience grief over the pain, the shame, and the permanent losses that cannot be brought back.

Third, we are flooded by *helplessness, powerlessness, and hopelessness*. These overwhelming emotions surge back and forth, hiding the sun of grace behind black clouds of stormy feelings.

I have found no special timetable for these stages. People may go back to the reporter stage because they can't tolerate the feelings. They may briefly escape into denial, only to come back out again. Sometimes when I explain these stages, someone will say, "I think I skipped one," or "I've been stuck in one too long."

My answer is, "Just work with the Lord and keep bringing your mind back to his truths. He will take you through the stages in the proper order and sequence. God wants you to find the right balance. He wants you to hate the sin and not the sinner. He wants you to learn to accept forgiveness for yourself, and to extend it to others. He wants you to realize that he is not to blame. All this takes time, sometimes a long time."

Bargaining away the past. We eventually move on beyond the feeling stage into the bargaining stage. That's when we say, "Well, this did happen but maybe I can get out of some of the consequences." Sad to say, the victim—the one who has been offended by the sin—is often the one who has to suffer through the ordeal of therapy.

Victims of childhood abuse can continue to live with the consequences of the past, forever confronting the residual problems. Or they can go through the painful process of therapy, work on their own behavior, grow and change. The very pain and struggle of turning around give us a new capability. Paul points out how good it was that Christ should suffer because it made him more fully able to relate to us and to comfort us in our suffering (2 Cor 1:4-5). The same is true of us. Once we have worked through our own pain, we can, in turn, comfort other people who suffer in a similar way. Our own process enables us to relate to them.

However, instead of seeing the process through, we often want to bargain and say, "OK, I'll admit that the past happened, and I'll look at it, but afterwards we'll make it all go away." By means of some little magic trick or slight of mind, we wish we could make it all go POOF. Unfortunately, no amount of insight can make unhealthy patterns of behavior disappear. Instead, with lots of support from the Lord and other Christians, we need to develop and practice new approaches to life. In doing so, the Lord's mercy is able to slowly turn around the consequences of past abuses.

Learning to accept. We then go on beyond our bargaining into a stage called acceptance. Acceptance does not mean saying that the sin was not so bad. Nor does it mean ignoring it or being resigned to it. Instead, we accept the fact that God is on the throne, and that he is good, righteous, and just. We accept our value as well as the value of those who have hurt us. We begin to see more fully how Christ died for us all. We accept and acknowledge the reality of other people's free will, and the fact that they may never choose to allow God to work in their lives.

We accept these things in the face of our powerlessness. Without God we can change nothing, but God can work all things together for good as we abide in him. And he pours out his infinite grace wherever sin abounds.

We accept God's offer to work with us, to give us the courage and strength to try to change ourselves, to allow him to change others. We accept the challenge of making ourselves available as tools in his hands to change the situation for the better. Most of all, we accept God's sovereignty. Believing that the fear of the Lord is the beginning of all wisdom, we choose to fear him.

Bringing good out of evil. Beyond acceptance we find an attitude very peculiar to Christians. After letting go of bitterness, after offering forgiveness, Christians can allow God to bring good out of evil. We are privileged to bring healing to the people who have wounded us. We choose to bring Christ's message and ministry into the very pain we've suffered.

If we will allow him to, God will bring us to the point where we can sit down and truly rejoice about what has happened to us. James sums up this attitude in calling upon believers to express joy in their suffering, knowing that they are going to benefit greatly from the discomfort (Jas 1:2-4).

I often hear a joke that goes around the church that really troubles me: "Don't ask God for patience, because he'll give you nothing but problems." Well, I think that's probably true. But what we're really saying is, "Oh, God gives you gifts all right, but he charges too much for them."

Let's remember James' advice.

WHAT IS FORGIVENESS?

God wants to bring good out of evil. He wants to heal those toward whom we feel bitter. To facilitate such healing, he requires us to forgive, just as he has forgiven us. But what is forgiveness, really? The devil loves to suggest an impossible definition of forgiveness and then beats us with guilt when we can't pull it off.

We may be equating forgiveness with things like trusting, excusing, and forgetting. We know all too well that we can't immediately turn around and trust someone who has hurt us. God certainly doesn't ask us to excuse that person's behavior. And we know we can never forget what's happened to us. So we end up crying out, "God, I just can't do what you want. It's impossible for me to forgive!"

To back up this approach, people sometimes quote the Scripture which says, "forgetting those things which are behind and reaching forward to those things which are ahead..." (Phil 3:13). Let's assume that this particular verse really means forgetting anything from the past which tries to keep us from pushing forward to whatever God has for us. That word "forgetting" still does not mean "never thinking about or never feeling

What forgetting really means is "neglecting, not dwelling upon, not going round and round about something which we cannot change."

When we first begin the grieving process we will feel our injury again and again, but as we grow, we'll begin to catch ourselves and be able to lay it aside without the same old bitterness. Later on, although specific events may trigger those same memories and certain occasions or anniversaries will bring up unpleasant feelings, our emotions will no longer keep us from obeying and serving God in the present.

Inevitable consequences. Another misconception about forgiveness is that there need be no consequences for misbehavior. Some well-known Christian leaders in the recent past have exemplified this mistaken notion. They have fallen into sin, apologized, and then immediately said, "If you're good Christians, you won't apply any consequences to my conduct. You'll forget about the whole thing and let me get back to my ministry."

These leaders aren't reading the same Bible as mine. I have a God who *always* applies consequences when we sin. He'll walk through those consequences with us, while using them to heal the wrong attitudes that caused us to sin in the first place. Sometimes God pours so much mercy upon repentant sinners that the consequences almost seem pleasurable. But life will never be what it would have been if we hadn't sinned in the first place.

As God treats us, we should treat one another. When someone has hurt you by wrongdoing of some kind, he or she may ask your forgiveness. If you truly love the person, you certainly will forgive. But you may also enroll your fellow sinner in the "consequences-as-best-teacher" school.

If you have to send somebody to jail, then do so. But write to them every day, visit every chance you get, and pray for them regularly. We love others when we set limits, apply consequences, and then walk through those consequences with them. It may prove to be the best thing that ever happened

Whom do you trust? We've also been led to believe that forgiveness means trusting people. I've heard it said so many times, "I said I'm sorry, so now you should trust me! You can't be much of a Christian if you don't trust me!"

Let's just start with one rather obvious fact. Who is the one person in the world you should *least* trust? Yourself! Don't trust yourself an inch; watch yourself like a hawk. You are always your own worst enemy. You'll come sneaking up on yourself and bash yourself over the head every time.

Logically, if we can't trust ourselves, why should we trust other people who have harmed us?

The only person we should ever trust is Christ living through others—when we can plainly see that they're letting him sit in the driver's seat, so to speak. We should bear in mind, however, that a person may very well grab the steering wheel away from Christ at any time, in which case we'd better get out of the way as fast as we can.

FINDING FRIENDS, BEING FRIENDS

How can we tell when someone is trustworthy, truly committed to Christ? Many people apologize when they get into trouble, but then turn right around and stab us in the back again. But what about the ones who really seem sincere in their repentance? Quite often, people who really are sorry still have no idea what it takes to follow through on their good intentions. And so they fall again.

What should we watch for in discerning trustworthiness in others? And in ourselves? For one thing people with whom we can feel safe freely admit that they've failed, but they don't dissolve into self-hatred on account of it. They accept forgiveness from God, offering neither excuses nor promises to be strong. Instead they reach out and try to bring healing where they've previously inflicted pain.

A real friend will also take the risk of telling us something we don't necessarily want to hear. They do this because they love us, along with the fact that they may battle the same pro

They are simply one beggar sharing with another beggar where the food is.

And what about us? Are we trustworthy and reliable? Safe people typically demonstrate four distinct qualities.

- First, trustworthy people will always ask themselves, "What is it about me that needs to change?" Safe people don't focus their attention on everybody else's faults and problems. They know they have plenty of their own.
- Second, trustworthy people always ask "How does this behavior measure up to the Word of God?" They will quickly admit that we are all too weak to change overnight, but they don't water down God's truths to make them more consoling.
- Third, these people affirm us, saying "Yes, you're doing well. And I agree that you need to move forward. Here are some suggestions as to how I think you could do so..." While they encourage and support us in positive ways, trustworthy people are also willing to make practical suggestions about how we can actually move from where we are to where we need to be.
- Fourth, and most importantly, safe people will seize opportunities to remind us, "You are valuable!" They will assure us that, no matter what our problem is, God will give us the power to cope with it, that our hope is secure in him.

Contrast this kind of person, for example, with those who often clobber us with a bunch of Bible verses. "Well, you're wrong, and the Bible makes it perfectly clear! God says it, I believe it, and that settles it!" they proclaim, arms firmly folded across the chest. What this person has to say might well be perfectly true, but the words leave the troubled listener feeling quite overwhelmed—and worthless.

In addition, these untrustworthy people never acknowledge their own weaknesses. Because we feel like such failures anyway, we assume that these folks must be living the Christian life perfectly or they wouldn't be sharing all those verses with us. The fact is, they've forgotten to tell us that they aren't able to obey God's Word any more than we are. They failed to mention that yes, they're trying with the Lord's help, but they have a long, long way to go. We're all in exactly the same boat.

We need to develop all four of those "safe person" qualities in our lives. It's equally important for us to look for them in others. God wants us to develop healthy relationships that will support our efforts to rely on God's grace.

True friends are willing to stick with us even when it costs them. Friends will see us through the worst of times as well as the best. They will walk arm in arm with us through our triumphs and our tragedies. Friends will reach out to us when we're too hurt to ask for help, and they'll leave us alone when we need a little space. Those with whom we can feel safe know us well, understand us better than we understand ourselves, and love us anyway.

The healing process I'm describing makes it more and more possible for such friends to become a part of our lives. Once we've worked through our past pain and abuse, we gradually become cleansed of the unhealthy behavior patterns that have alienated us from others. Our defenses drop. Our personality disorders diminish.

- We forgive and receive forgiveness.
- We dare to love and we receive love.
- We choose to be a friend and we receive friendship.

Our focus is no longer on ourselves and our endless quest for value, power, or hope. As we give up our pride, we are able to let God be God in our lives. We soon will find him to be the most wonderful, powerful Friend of all. And we also find that God is able to work with failures. He will turn our past destructive patterns of behavior around. He will allow his strength to be perfected in our weakness.

Return to Relationship

A RADIANT BRIDE CLOTHED in white satin and pearls, Jane glowed with happiness as she swept down the church aisle on her father's arm. He had spared no expense on the occasion, even going beyond the call of duty in making the wedding ceremony and reception especially lavish.

The young couple's engagement, like most, had been a rather unrealistic period of time. Jane and Tom had lived in a happy fantasy of dreams and dates, with little cause for conflict or controversy. They had envisioned a charming house, stylish furniture, romantic holidays, trips abroad, and happy reunions with college friends. And they had focused a great deal of attention on the wedding preparations.

But the honeymoon brought their sweet fantasy to an abrupt end. On their wedding night, Jane was unable to deal with the intimacies of marriage. Every time Tom drew her close, she automatically recoiled. Mystifying images of her father's face and vague memories of his hands on her body caused the young bride to withdraw from her groom in terror. Jane felt shaken and physically sick. Tom felt rejected. Their romantic expectations had been deeply disappointed.

A year after the wedding Jane came to see me for counseling. She was a devastated woman after battling these painful dilemmas with no success. Why was she having horrible visions of her father mistreating her sexually? Why couldn't she respond to her loving husband's desire to hold her close? Was she sexually abnormal? Was she losing her mind?

Jane had simply cut herself off from her father to avoid dealing with these haunting questions. The rest of her family bombarded her with questions. "What's wrong between you and dad? Why are you treating him like this? You're breaking his heart—you know how much he's always loved you!"

After weeks of unrelenting interrogation, Jane began tentatively to bring up the memories she was having. She told her sister. She tried to talk to her mother. Both of them accused her of fabricating the stories. They thought she was a terrible person for even mentioning such things.

"That couldn't possibly have happened, Jane!" her mother snapped, storming out of the room.

"And even if it did," her sister continued, "it was years ago. Why can't you just forgive and forget? You're making everyone miserable! What's wrong with you, Jane?"

After two or three weeks of unpleasant conversations both in her presence and behind her back, Jane was asked by her brother whether she would consider forgiving her father if he apologized. The young bride hated the thought of such a confrontation, but talked it over with Tom, who had been wonderfully supportive of her throughout the ordeal. She agreed. "Fine. If he's willing to talk about it, so am I."

One afternoon, the family gathered in the parent's living room. Jane's father twisted a handkerchief in his hands. His eyes looked plaintive. Her mother's face was pinched and tense. The older woman's expression seemed to plead, "Why are we going through all this? What a troublemaker you are, Jane."

The room grew quiet after Jane and Tom sat down. Jane waited. This was the moment that could change the course of her life, her relationship with her father, her family's future, maybe even her marriage.

Her father took a deep breath, fidgeted in his chair, and

looked at his shoes. At last he spoke.

"Well Jane, I'm sorry for whatever I may have done so long ago. I'm sorry for whatever it was that caused you to shut me out like this...."

As far as Jane was concerned, this last betrayal was worse than all the rest. She simply could not receive such an empty apology. She rose to her feet, weeping. Tom stood at her side. Without another word, they left the room.

Although Jane finally received healing from Christ and is now able to enjoy a happy and fulfilling marriage, she has done so without any repentance from her father. Without a word of sincere apology. And without any support from her family. Her climb out of despair was long and painful, when it could have been an occasion for deep reconciliation and reunion.

THE POWER OF PARDON

We continue to deal with bitterness by a return to relationship. As we work toward healthier relationships with friends and loved ones, we will inevitably have to deal with the issue of apology—both giving and receiving pardon for past hurts. We want to be more trustworthy, as well as to be able to trust other people in our lives. Apologies are an important factor in establishing those resilient relationships.

Jesus provides an ideal model for apology when he tells the story about the prodigal son in Luke 15. Like most of us, this young man had to hit bottom before he was able to seek reconciliation with his father. It's amazing how far people have to fall before they hit bottom. Here is a rich, pampered landowner's son who is eating leftover pig cuisine—garbage—before he realizes that he needs to apologize, make amends, and get his life straightened out.

Jesus tells us that, eventually, the prodigal son came to his senses. Then he carefully worked out in his mind the steps of a proper apology. It's interesting to note that he never even got to finish his whole apology. His father, seeing his son's good attitude and intention, swiftly forgave him and took him back in.

But that was the father's choice.

Let's look at the *steps in apology* the prodigal son saw as necessary in restoring his relationship.

1. God is convicting me of my wrong attitude of _____.
2. Which caused me to hurt you by_____.
3. I can only guess what it was like for you. Would you let me make amends by_____?
4. Because I don't want to hurt you again, I'm obtaining support and accountability through_____.
5. I'm not asking you to risk a relationship with me because I'm worthy. If I were in your shoes, after the way I've treated you, I'd be hesitant.
6. Maybe we could start by taking a small risk and building only as I demonstrate responsibility. I need your friendship.
7. Would you now forgive me?

Try working through these same steps in your own mind in regard to someone with whom you need to be reconciled. Be specific about the details of your own circumstances. Don't include any of the other person's part in the matter. Don't make excuses. And don't promise to be strong.

"Father, I have sinned," said the prodigal. The first rule is never to be vague. Sometimes people come to us and say, "Well, I'm sorry for whatever it is I did to make you so irritable." Let me try to translate that into everyday English for you: "I am so wonderful that I'm willing to apologize to you for things too small for normal people to detect. You are such a monster that you require apologies for slights that no one in his right mind would even notice." That kind of an apology is an attack, not an apology.

Be specific about the offenses you know you have committed and never include the other person's part. We try to mention their contribution to the problem because we want to minimize what we ourselves have done. However, whenever we try to make an apology less painful for ourselves, our efforts will end up ruining its effectiveness. Apologies are God's favorite behavior modification technique. He wants them to hurt, so that the next time we're about to make mistakes we'll remember how uncomfortable we were and consequently have second thoughts.

When we're apologizing we need to say things like, "God is convicting me of my bad attitude of inferiority. Greed. Bitterness. Sensuality. Hypocrisy." What was it that drove you to act badly in this particular relationship? Get in touch with the specific attitudes and confess them. Then the person to whom you are apologizing knows that you're not just dealing with offenses, but with the underlying attitudes that motivated them.

David says to the Lord, "Against you, you only, have I sinned, And done this evil in your sight" (Ps 51:4). If we don't take care of our sin against God, we aren't getting to the heart of the matter. After doing so, we need to move on and say, "My bad attitude, which is a sin against God, has caused me to hurt you. It has caused me to do things that brought loss into your life."

MAKING AMENDS

We may need to make some amends, which has nothing to do with trying to pay for the past. You can't do that—it's impossible. The past is gone and cannot be brought back. The hurt, the destroyed relationship, the loneliness, the problems that stemmed from the sin—none of that can be brought back. So what's the point of making amends?

Making amends deals with the *present* consequences of what we may have done in the past. If we stole something, the Scriptures say that we don't just pay it back. We do two things: we pay back more than what we took and we establish a permanent pattern of giving to those in need. (We'll learn more about that later.)

Perhaps nothing was stolen. Maybe we spoke abusively— called someone a jerk or an idiot. Perhaps we said, "What's the matter with you? Why can't you do anything right?" Some of us have accumulated a hundred thousand such comments over the years. That leaves a huge debt to pay—which is counted in multiplied thousands of *positive* comments. Thus making amends may well take us the rest of our lives.

Our apology ought to include this sort of statement, "An attitude of inferiority caused me to put you down, and it was wrong. I'd like to point out that the truth is that you are sensitive, caring, hard-working..." We are instructed by God to build where we've torn down and to exhort where we once destroyed.

My wife and I once welcomed a new Christian into our home. This man desperately needed a place to stay for a couple of weeks until he could get permanently settled and stabilized. At the time, we were involved with a mission church in inner city Detroit.

The man, like so many others in his position, had developed problems with substance abuse and was trying in his own strength to overcome them. The man repaid our hospitality by stealing my wife's sewing machine. In our eyes, it wasn't *our* machine anyway—it belonged to God. But we were grieved by the loss of relationship. Meanwhile, he pawned it for a fraction of its value.

About a year later I was surprised to receive a phone call from this same man. "The Lord has convicted me," he explained. "I've confessed my sin to him and now I want to apologize to you." The man apologized, but never once did he offer to pay so much as a dollar a month for the sewing machine. He did not attempt to make amends of any kind for what he did.

Of course there was no way that he could have ever paid us back for the sadness that his theft brought into our own home, or for the difficult feelings that we had to fight within ourselves. Eventually the Lord took care of the loss and rewarded us with another sewing machine. But, because the man didn't even try to make any amends, I knew that he was not truly repentant. He was not someone with whom we could take risks.

It's important for us to remember that none of us is worthy, apart from God's grace. So often Christians say to each other, "Because you are a Christian you should forgive me," or "Yes, I hurt you, but after all I have done for you, you should forgive me," or "It's your fault I sinned, so you have to forgive me."

Truly repentant believers never try to prove that they deserve forgiveness. It would be more appropriate if they said, "If I were in your shoes I sure would have a lot of trouble forgiving me. But if you would, I would sure appreciate it."

And a word to the wise—if someone says to you, "I promise—I'll never do it again!" watch out. Those kinds of statements indicate that these people don't understand their powerlessness. It is virtually certain that they will repeat their offense.

Beth's father was a pastor. "Such a wonderful, godly, kind man," she would often hear people say about him. It was hard for her to listen to those compliments without feeling deep, surging emotions. She knew those words weren't at all true, but there was nothing she could do about it.

Beth's father happened to be a very violent man in the privacy of his home. Wanting his "preacher's kids" to behave in ways that would make him proud, he enforced every house rule with a vengeance. Whatever weapon he used for his beating, he used with all his might. The next day, the bruises were carefully hidden from the rest of the world. But they still hurt, and hurt badly.

But that wasn't the worst of it. Beth's father not only beat her; he sexually molested her on a regular basis. Sometimes, when her mother was away from home, he even took her out of school to meet his insatiable, perverse cravings.

But, come Sunday morning, Beth's father was a different man. In the pulpit he was eloquent. He was charming. He had a captivating personality as a minister, which kept him surrounded by adoring church members. No one could have imagined his "other" self. The man seemed to have a split personality that admitted, only rarely, that maybe—just maybe— he had a problem.

Once in a while he told Beth, "I'm sorry to take you out of school. You know, I'm going to have to stop doing this." Other times he said, "I'm sorry if I hit you a little hard, but it's for your own good." Of course, as a child, Beth thought he was sincere. She thought he would stop. She thought he was repentant. And in her innocence she forgave him—again and again and again.

Beth felt very confused by her father's apparent godliness and by his constant apologies. Was she doing something wrong to cause the incidents to continue? Did she deserve the severe beatings? Was she somehow encouraging the sexual molestation?

As an adult, Beth's perplexity extended beyond the details of her abuse into the very heart of Christianity. Her father represented the gospel, the good news of Jesus Christ. He was a pastor, a Christian leader, a beloved member of the community. When Beth thought about the holiness of God, she was filled with confusion and cynicism. But when she contemplated forgiveness and repentance, her skepticism was immense. Mistrust had seized every fiber of her being.

REBUILDING RELATIONSHIPS

In trying to offer an apology, someone may say, "I'll tell you what. I'll go away and never bother you again." They're trying to render some payment for their sins. Instead of bailing out, a more productive offer would be to suggest some basis on which to rebuild the broken relationship. The prodigal son planned to ask his father if he could return as a household servant. On other occasions, people want to jump right back into the relationship, as if nothing had ever happened. They want to carry on without taking the time or making the effort to change what may be deep-rooted, dangerous habits.

Let's say that a husband has a pattern of losing his temper and striking his wife. At her request, this man has moved out of the house. After a short time he feels ready to apologize and make amends. He shouldn't say, "Look, I've been to therapy three times. I've learned a couple of things and I promise to never do it again."

Instead he might tell his wife, "Even if you were to take me back this very instant, I'd be afraid to come home. I know my weakness and I'm trying to get in touch with God's strength inside of me. I suggest that we meet with a counselor once a week, and maybe go to church together once a week. If that goes OK then we could try praying together. If that goes OK maybe we could go on a date once a week. If that goes OK maybe I can come over each evening and we could do things together. If that goes OK then maybe I could move back in."

The very willingness to work at restoring a relationship step-by-step goes a long way toward making the other person feel more comfortable. If we happen to be the ones who have been wronged, we also need to be sensitive enough to guide a repentant person toward taking the proper steps. When someone offers a glib apology, we might respond, "I appreciate your spirit of repentance. I have found in my own life that when I repent of something, I need to admit I'm powerless, get in touch with my underlying attitude, make amends, and allow God time to do his work."

We can then suggest to that person the steps I outlined earlier in this chapter. If he or she agrees to go along with the process, we can feel sure that person is truly repentant, but was uninformed as to how to apologize. What if the answer is "Yes, but...," followed by a resistance to the steps? That person is only penitent about the *consequences* rather than the sin itself. In this case, we should be wary and wear our bullet-proof vest lest we get shot in the back again. Someone may have the best of intentions and never dream of hurting us again. Such a person may believe he or she won't, but lack the power not to.

HOW TO INSPIRE OTHERS TO CHANGE

We often use bitterness to safeguard ourselves from further pain in relationships, but there are better means of protection. God has given us some biblical influence techniques—ways to be involved with all kinds of people, both trustworthy and untrustworthy, truly sorry or unrepentant. These measures protect us while they release God's power into their lives.

Before we proceed to take a look at those ways of inspiring others to change, let me first ask you a question. Let's say that God gives you a concern, a burden, a focus on someone else, and you want to see them change. Where does he always begin? What does he suggest should be your starting point? I'm sure you know the answer: work on yourself.

Boy, that is so irritating. I've tried to talk God out of it so many times. I've said, "Lord, this is a difficult situation. I'm trying to help a person and they don't want to change. How do I increase the chance they will change?"

The Lord says, "Well, Verle, I've been meaning to talk to you about some things—things you're doing and things you need to work on."

"But Lord, you didn't hear me. There's this person over here that I'm trying to change. How do I change them?"

The Lord says, "I did hear you. And there are some things I want to talk to *you* about."

God always brings it back to me. And he seems very stubborn about this point. He starts dealing with my insides—my attitudes as well as my actions. Then when I turn around and try to make the other person change first, he'll say, "Back off."

When we set behavioral limits on other people, we aren't supposed to concern ourselves with their attitudes. That's the Holy Spirit's job. We can certainly pray for them, but our focus should be on sharing ideas, modeling behavior, setting up boundaries, and clarifying consequences.

What do we do when our minds start to focus on, "Yes, but they don't understand… they don't appreciate… they don't cooperate…"? We have to remember that the way they *feel* is between them and God. The limits we set can only concern the things they *do*. God changes hearts, not us. That's way out of our league.

Meanwhile, what is it about our own actions and attitudes that could use some attention? Where should we begin to work on those things over which we do have some control? As we ourselves are changed, we are more and more able to inspire change in the lives of those around us.

Affirming grace. Our first step in influencing others to change is to affirm grace—to place value on the other person as well as on ourselves. We need to remain calm and confident. God calls us to live life with abundance and invite others to join in.

By "abundance," I mean growing in our relationship with the Lord, storing up treasure in heaven, allowing him to work through us, becoming more like Christ, bringing God glory, and benefiting others. And no matter what other people do, we continue to pray for them while we maintain our own walk with God. God is the one who has to change them. If we allow ourselves to hate them, we will become like the person we hate. Even if you set all the other limits right, if you remain uptight and angry inside, your relationship will never change.

It's obviously important not to reward people for bad behavior. Whether we respond negatively or positively to their manipulation, we are probably giving them what they want—power to make us react. Instead, let's reward people when they act in accordance to God's will. Let's encourage them, bless them, and give them affirmation for behavior that will bring forth God's best in their lives—for their sake and for ours.

Praying for troublemakers. Jesus instructed us to pray for those who despitefully use us. Pray for what? A good place to start is the prayer that Christ prayed on the cross: "Father, forgive them for they know not what they do." Do you think maybe Jesus was just being nice and giving them the benefit of the doubt? Was he perhaps a little dehydrated and delusional? Of course not. Jesus meant what he said.

What if you were to say about the people who've hurt you, "God forgive them, they didn't really understand"? Your mind would probably be objecting all the while, "Oh, yes they did!" And on one level, the people who put Christ on the cross knew exactly what they were doing. They knew that he was going to die. They certainly knew that crucifixion was shameful and agonizing.

Jesus knew that the Pharisees wanted him to die in pain, that they were jealous and bitter. The high priest had pronounced it expedient for one man to die for the people. Yet even so, those who wanted to crucify Jesus did not see fully who he was or what they were doing.

In part the religious leaders had convinced themselves that they were protecting the Jewish faith and preventing a Roman slaughter of the Hebrews. They hated this man who claimed to be the Son of God and indignantly rejected him as a blasphemer. In doing so, they rejected the revelation of God and offered proof of their own blindness, rebellion, and pride.

The Roman soldiers were used to the grisly scene of crucifixion. Even though they may have harbored no personal reasons for putting this man to death, they acted despitefully toward Jesus, shaming him and spitting on him and reviling him. So what did Jesus mean by his prayer of forgiveness? He meant that although those who condemned him to the cross thought they had a good reason for killing him, they did not understand who he was and what was the real significance of his death. Those who nailed Jesus to the cross had no idea what they were actually doing: crucifying the very Son of God. Jesus recognized that all of these people were unaware of the magnitude of their sin—blinded, sinful, wretched, and pitifully unaware. Jesus did not excuse their sin but asked God to forgive them for their own sake.

In today's world, the situation is much the same. I have observed again and again that most people who hurt others do not understand the full impact of what they're doing. They even convince themselves they have a good reason for their behavior. So we have to pray with Jesus, "Father forgive them. They don't really understand." It is so healing for us to follow his example. Realizing that our enemies are self-blinded, we can ask God's mercy upon them for their own sake. Forgiveness is a gift we give ourselves. It brings relief, joy, and life to us and maybe even to the other person.

Have mercy on them, Lord. The next thing we need to pray is that God will have mercy on those who hurt us. This is a hard prayer, because deep inside we want to cry out, "God, why are you taking so long to make them pay?" We really long to see them suffer for what they've done. Our human nature wants to teach them some hard lessons.

But the Bible says, "The goodness of God leads you to repentance" (Rom 2:4). When God's mercy and kindness lead people to repentance, we need to thank him for his mercy. Besides, when we are the ones who have caused others pain, we ourselves cry out for mercy, don't we? God hears us and helps us. Why should he do less for our enemies?

Please open their eyes. We may even feel led to ask God to lay a heavy hand upon those who have hurt us as a way of opening their eyes. We might pray something like this: "Lord, take away their peer support. Make others stop giving confirmation of their actions. Cause the bartender to get bored. Get the women at the office to say, 'Your wife doesn't understand you? Well neither do we! How come you're always whining? Whine, whine, whine! It's a wonder she puts up with you as much as she does....'" You get the idea.

We can also pray, "Lord, take away the temporary rewards of sin." A lot of times we forget that sin brings pleasure. Sin brings relief. Sin brings a sense of power. To clarify this point, let's look at an obvious sin, the one that probably causes the most frequent and horrible damage: inappropriate sexual relationships. God created sex to be pleasurable. He intends it for our good and the good of the human race. Then the devil comes along and says that we can get this pleasure on our own timetable without any responsibility

So when we pray for somebody, ask God to take the pleasure out of the action. When the sin occurs, the sinner will gain no pleasure, no relief, no sense of power. And that sin will seem exceedingly sinful, indeed. That in itself can be a powerful incentive to repent.

So we can ask God to bring discomfort into the lives of those who need to change. But if he does, we should be prepared to meet their needs. And we should check our own motivations. We shouldn't rejoice when God begins to bring trouble into their lives, saying, "It's about time!" We can recognize that it may be necessary for God to stir them up, but we should seek their best interests.

RECOGNIZING THE POWER OF PRAYER

Catherine started praying these prayers for her husband. Not a Christian himself, he desperately needed to change some of his behavior patterns. After a couple of weeks, she came back to me and said, "Maybe I shouldn't say those prayers anymore."

"Why not?" I could see that she was feeling some distress.

Catherine hesitated and then explained, "Well, my husband has his own business. Ever since I started praying this way, he's been losing contracts. And hasn't got any new ones. We're running out of money, and I don't know how we're going to pay our bills. If this kind of thing continues, we'll lose the house and we're certainly going to lose the business."

One thing became obvious to both of us. When we pray life-changing prayers about people close to us, we may have to suffer when they do. When God begins to convict people they may thrash around. They may become deeply disturbed. They may become unpleasant to be around. And yet we can't stop being involved with them.

I couldn't help but smile. "It sounds like you think you are nicer than God, Catherine. Do you think God is being any meaner than he has to be?"

God is never mean or vindictive, of course, but he lovingly designs experiences that are sufficiently disturbing to catch people's attention. We are all so blind! Like the prodigal son we usually have to hit bottom, and bottom can be pretty low. Our loving involvement with people can soften them up and prepare them for God's intervention.

It's also important that we ask God to have mercy on people when we ask him to intervene in their lives. We know that only the Lord can find the perfect balance of mercy and justice.

Sometimes we look at all the problems of life, throw our hands up and say, "Oh God, there's not a thing I can do!" We feel worthless, helpless, and bitter. But the Word of God promises that we *can* do something. We can release the power of the Holy Spirit into the situation. We can apologize for our part in the problem and make amends. We can ask God to change us in the same ways the other person needs to change. And then we can pray, not with the attitude, "Oh well, there's nothing else I can do... I guess I can pray," but with confidence in prayer's power. I find that when we pray in these ways, with the understanding that our prayers are powerful, our bitterness melts away.

Prayer is profoundly significant. And prayer prepares us to set distinct boundaries around ourselves. Boundaries, established on the basis of God's Word, help us live our lives without the ungodly defenses we've always counted on for self-protection. Learning to draw lines in this way is never easy. The next chapter will provide some tools for doing this in your own life.

7 | Learning to Draw the Line

THE SEVEN-YEAR-OLD BOY sat in the corner busily playing with some toys. A more careful observer might have noticed his brown eyes darting furtively around the cluttered bedroom, subtly betraying the fact that his mind really wasn't on having fun. Davy was actually working very hard at giving his mother that impression, pretending that he hadn't a care in the world.

His mother stood at the bedroom door scowling, her arms folded, her body tense with irritation. Jackie looked around her son's messy room and fixed her attention on his unmade bed. Just as she suspected, the boy had disobeyed her—again.

Davy and Jackie were having a contest of wills. Each of them had a different outcome in mind: Jackie's goal was to get the boy to make his bed; Davy's goal was to make his mother mad and thereby gain power over her.

Mother and son used different techniques in trying to accomplish their own objectives. Jackie's angry words spilled out, "I work long and hard at my job and I am not your slave! You should appreciate everything I do for you. I buy your food and clothes and if it weren't for me, you'd be living on the street! I've told you a million times to make your bed. Can't you help me around here even a little bit, Davy?"

Jackie was trying to make her son feel bad by going after his insides. Recognizing her utter frustration, Davy knew that he had already won the battle over the bed. He searched his mind for the perfect, winning technique. He realized that he was too small to threaten his mother, but that wouldn't work very well anyway. Since she was already playing the martyr game, he sensed that he couldn't compete with her martyrdom. So the boy decided to use "space out." As his mother yelled at him he looked off, out the window, and just let his mind drift. His eyelids fluttered a little. A dreamy expression drifted across his face.

Jackie was infuriated. She commanded, "You look at me when I'm talking to you. You listen to me!"

The boy turned slowly around, his expression studiedly blank and innocent. "Why you little...!" Jackie freaked out and started slapping him. Davy had won. The bed still wasn't made and his mother was mad.

Where did Jackie go wrong in dealing with her son? Her problem was focusing on the boy's motivations or attitudes. Instead, she should have said something like this: "Look Davy, here's the deal. If that bed isn't made when this timer goes off, you're going to sit in your chair for fifteen minutes, facing the wall. If you do make the bed, you can play with Ryan for half an hour before you do your homework."

By calmly asserting herself, Jackie could have scored a major victory: Davy could no longer be rewarded for making his mother miserable. He would recognize a clear choice—good consequences for good behavior, bad consequences for bad behavior. Under the circumstances, Davy might as well go ahead and make the bed. It would only take a minute anyway.

What does Scripture have to say about learning to draw the line? As we discuss several verses in this chapter, you may begin to rethink what it means to be meek and humble. These are some techniques for godly assertiveness. These are ways in which any of us, with God's help, can take the initiative in a situation.

CARING FOR CULPRITS

As we discussed in the previous chapter, your job is not to control other people but to release the Lord into the situation.

In doing so, God needs to borrow your face, your mouth, your tongue, your hands, and your body to work through.

Jesus referred to an Old Testament passage which reads "If your enemy is hungry, feed him; if he is thirsty, give him something to drink" (Prv 25:21-22). Perhaps you've heard Scriptures like that one explained away in some book or sermon. Maybe you've been told that this principle is only an elusive ideal we can't be expected to reach in this earthly life. Or that this teaching is intended for another place or another time.

I firmly disagree. I believe that today, in the here and now, the Lord expects us to meet the practical needs of the people who have hurt us. And we are to do so, whether they appreciate it or not, whether they change or not. The results are in God's hands. The trying is ours. Our reward is from God not from the person to whom we minister.

If you ask God, he will give you opportunities to meet the needs of your enemies, or at least to care for the culprits who can make your life miserable in more subtle ways. He will especially want you to do so when he starts bringing discomfort into their lives. In their discomfort, they will develop needs that you can meet. And when you meet those needs, God will take away your own bitterness. Investing in the life of an enemy is one of the most powerful techniques available for getting rid of bitterness.

Remember one rule here, however. You don't want to meet a practical need that will damage the other person. Let's say the friend who has hurt you is an alcoholic who begs for a fifth of whiskey to avoid delirium tremors. You aren't going to give him that fifth of whiskey. You can give him something to eat. You can provide him with some vitamins. You can take him somewhere to get help. But you have to refuse to directly fuel his problem.

Let me share a very powerful example of this principle being put into action. Doug and Marge had one daughter, the only child God had given them. Although they had wanted more children, Mary was a delight and they were grateful for her. Their pride and joy grew up to be a godly young lady and went off to college. She was on the honor roll, enthusiastically working her way toward medical school.

One night Mary's roommate called her parents. Mary wasn't in the dormitory and the girl was worried. She asked if Mary was at home with them. Doug intuitively sensed that something was terribly wrong. "No, she's not here. She's supposed to be there at school. When was the last time you saw her?"

And so the tragedy unfolded. Doug called the police and received a disinterested reply: "Oh well, you know how kids are. She's probably off with her boyfriend."

Doug and Marge knew very well that Mary wasn't with a boy—she didn't even have a boyfriend. But the police refused to start searching for her until another forty-eight hours had passed. The distraught parents began to get angry. They knew, deep inside, that Mary was a victim of somebody, somewhere.

Eventually, their instincts proved to be correct. A lengthy, disheartening manhunt followed. After several weeks the parents' remaining hopes were shattered. Countless prayers were answered with a resounding no. Mary was found dead.

Before long, the police caught the man who had killed Mary. When the indictment went to trial, no grisly details were spared. As they sat weeping through the proceedings, Doug and Marge's minds were filled with the violent details of what had happened to their beloved daughter. Bitterness overtook them both. Before long they couldn't get along with each other, and their marriage seemed headed for divorce.

To date, four lives had been destroyed: Mary's, the killer's, Doug's, and Marge's. The two parents went to their pastor for help in dealing with their bitterness against God. Seeing no possible escape from their misery, they asked, "What do we do now?" really without hope of an answer.

The pastor studied them carefully before responding to their desperate plea. Then he spoke, almost hesitantly. "Well, what I have to ask you to do is going to sound very unreasonable. You're not going to like it at all. But if you want to get rid of the bitterness in your hearts, you must invest in the life of the man who killed your daughter."

Doug and Marge immediately rebelled at the very thought. That man was a worthless murderer. What did he deserve except the full extent of the law: capital punishment! They struggled with the pastor's advice for quite a while but eventually decided to try. After all, what did they have to lose? They drove to the prison, realizing that they didn't have a clue as to how to reach out to the man.

Finally, after consulting with the warden, they concluded that the only thing they could do was to put money into the man's canteen account. The prison had a little store where inmates could buy soap, combs, and candy bars. Mary's killer didn't have a dime in the world. So Doug and Marge agreed to make a small financial gift toward his purchases.

They continued to do this for several weeks. Eventually they met with the man. When they explained their mission to him, he was deeply moved. He felt so overwhelmed by the powerful witness of their Christian faith in action that Doug and Marge were able to lead him to the Lord. His unexpected conversion inspired them to begin a prison ministry.

Today, hundreds of inmates' lives have been turned around by this couple's willingness to love their enemy. Nothing could make Mary's death good or right or anything less than tragic. The horror of losing her will stay with Doug and Marge for the rest of their lives. But their bitterness disappeared the moment they first put a little money in the murderer's canteen account.

WALKING MILE NUMBER TWO

In addition to meeting people's practical needs and investing in their lives, Jesus also advised "When your enemy forces you to walk one mile with him and carry his load, walk two instead." There is a very good reason for walking that second mile. You see, many people in our daily lives want to control us in one way or another in order to accomplish their own agenda. They may do it by trying to fight with us, to manipulate us, or to stir us up emotionally. Walking the second mile is God's technique for taking back control of our own lives.

During the time of Christ, Roman soldiers used the town of Joppa as a seaport. After docking their boats, they would shoulder their heavy packs and weaponry, then set out from Joppa to walk up the foothills and into the mountains toward the Jerusalem garrison. In order to make this long, hard trip easier for the Roman soldiers, a law was passed that they could require young Hebrew boys to carry their packs for one mile.

The Jewish people vehemently hated this law. It was bad enough that the Romans were controlling the adults. Couldn't they leave their children alone? It was one of the most hated laws in the country, something people were always complaining about. One day the Lord gathered those beleaguered Hebrew boys around himself and said, "The next time one of those Roman soldiers makes you go one mile with him, tell him you'll go two miles."

Can you imagine the shock on their faces? Those boys probably looked at each other and shook their heads. "This is one crazy rabbi! We thought he was going to tell us how to get out of going the first mile. Now he wants us to go twice as far!" But consider the difference such a free-will offer would make. If those boys decided at the very beginning to walk two miles instead of one, their bitterness would evaporate. They would be in control of the situation.

Let's see if we can apply this same principle to our everyday lives. I would state it this way: when someone forces you to do something, as long as it isn't wrong, do even more than he asks—with a good attitude.

I've run into so many people who say, "Dr. Bell, you don't understand. I've walked the hundredth mile." What they mean is that they have put up with an awful lot and it has been a real strain. I agree with them, but they're not walking any *second* miles. They're walking a whole bunch of first miles—one after the other. They keep getting caught and forced to walk that *first* mile over and over again and they keep putting up with it. And of course they feel the strain.

I remember a time when I had been working with a group of teenaged boys for several months. I wasn't sure how much of my message was getting across to them. Sometimes I would look for situations in their lives to which God's principles could be applied, even though it was obvious that they weren't particularly interested in my ideas. Those teenagers laughed at my "foolish" ideas, and sometimes they looked at me like I was completely crazy. The only reason the boys attended the group meeting at all was because their parents made them.

One of the boys was a rather bright lad who genuinely seemed to grasp God's truths in his heart. His father had trouble with alcohol and could be quite abusive at times. One Saturday afternoon Peter was watching television in his room. He had been sitting there all day long and his dad was thoroughly annoyed. He came charging into the room, snapped off the TV set and yelled, "Peter! Clean your room! It looks like a tornado hit it. Why do you have to be such a slob? Are you going to live like this for the rest of your life? Why should your mother and I have to look at that mess?"

The teenager began to react in the normal adolescent manner: "Who does he think he is, telling me what to do? What kind of father is he anyhow? He's never around, and when he does show up, he's either drunk or he's yelling at me. Besides, he waited until my favorite program was on—just to make me mad!"

Then the Holy Spirit suddenly broke through to Peter and reminded him of what I had said at the group meeting about walking the second mile: "Sounds like a second mile situation to me. It's not wrong to clean your room. Your dad is big enough to make you. Maybe you should do *more* than he asked."

Peter was wonderfully creative. He jumped up, made his bed, and shoved it into the middle of the room. He picked up all the things on the floor and put them away. Then he took some old newspapers and covered everything, found a gallon of paint in the garage, and proceeded to paint his bedroom. After the walls had dried, he moved everything back where it belonged. Peter felt pretty impressed with himself. He called up his friends and invited them over to see his room. He enjoyed the rest of the day. And, most significantly, Peter didn't have a trace of bitterness left inside.

His parents were impressed, too. In fact, the next time they brought him in for therapy they said, "You know what Peter did? Just out of the blue he painted his room." If anyone can force you to do what you don't want to, (as long as it isn't sinful) choose to do even more, with a good attitude, learning all you can.

TURNING THE OTHER CHEEK

Are you beginning to see the power of choosing to do things God's way? His methods always work, even though they go against the grain. For example, Jesus said, "And to him who strikes on the one cheek, offer the other also" (Lk 6:29). This verse is often used to excuse our putting up with abuse. In fact, it is a way of setting limits! Jesus didn't say to open up your whole body and psyche for injury; he said to make a free choice not to angrily defend ourselves but rather to humbly endure an unjust attack.

How should we respond when we are attacked? Our enemies expect one of several things to happen. They expect us to defend ourselves, to counterattack, to run away, to freeze, or to tuck our tail between our legs and say, "Poor me. I'm miserable. I'm worthless. You win." Then when we've provided them with more ammunition, they attack by saying that we're defensive, nasty, cowardly, or wimpish.

Once again, when you're attacked by surprise, you're dealing with a control issue. The people who attack us are counting on either escalation or complete victory. They have planned out at least their initial moves and feel in control. But God wants to grab hold of the situation and he needs to use our words and actions to do it. He wants us to use a technique that they aren't expecting—to gather information and seek solutions.

When we're attacked—especially out of the blue—we have to roll with the punches long enough to figure out where the other person is coming from. What is his or her need or goal? Only then can we seek effective solutions. If the attacks are pre-dictable and constant, then I believe that we seek the best inter-ests of our attacker by gathering support and by drawing the line: "No, you may not do that."

Don't be troubled if the godly response is so alien to you that you have to be somewhat mechanical in your response. So often we want healthy, godly responses to just bubble out of us like an effervescent spring. But that's not reasonable. We have to prac-tice to learn a new behavior.

Unfortunately, people may further deride us for being mechanical. "That's not the real you." But don't be dissuaded.

Better to be mechanically right than spontaneously wrong. We have to take the time to avoid an emotional reaction in our efforts to apply God's technique to the situation. Once we carry it out, he will bless the effort—and we'll become able to accomplish this more quickly the more we practice.

As is the case with most therapists, I am verbally attacked frequently. I remember one incident in the middle of a group session. One of the women was having trouble understanding and remembering my teaching that day and she felt I was giving her too much to do. She attacked me and said, "Dr. Bell, you're just proud and arrogant. You act like you think you're superior to everybody else."

Naturally, I wanted to defend myself and strike out at her. But I knew that wasn't what the Lord wanted to do. Since I don't belong to myself, I had to figure out how to yield myself to Christ—my thoughts, my words, my gestures. I reminded myself of the message I was always teaching. *I guess I had better practice what I preach*, I silently reminded myself.

Then I thought, *This is an attack and I'm supposed to turn the other cheek. I don't get to defend myself or attack her. But, on the other hand, I'm certainly not going to just dump on myself. Let me think—where is she coming from? Maybe she has a point. Maybe I do need to examine myself.*

I felt I needed further information, so I politely inquired, "Could you give me some feedback? What exactly are you saying? Tell me what I say and do that seems arrogant."

This woman began to point out some things. As I listened, I could see some room for improvement on my part. However, to some extent she was just reacting to me because she didn't like the truth.

While I listened I considered various solutions. I suggested that maybe I could communicate in a more effective way. Perhaps I could take more time, write things down, ask more questions. She thought maybe that would be helpful.

This proved to be an interesting experience. By the end of that hour the woman had actually changed her mind. I didn't *have* to defend myself. If I had given in to my first emotional reaction, she might have gone around town saying, "That Dr. Bell is so defensive!"

The only way to gain control in a situation like that is to roll with the punches. Turning the other cheek isn't an idealistic, impractical concept. It is a very sound, very sensible idea which can yield stellar results.

MAKING AN APPEAL

Another valuable and godly technique that proves to be a very helpful tool is making an appeal. This is something you can do when you want people to consider changing the way they're trying to accomplish something. Let me give you a suggested format. (Warning: you may not like these steps, but give them a try; you will like the results.)

1. *I appreciate your positive goal of*_____.
   This statement gives the other person the benefit of the doubt in the situation. Instead of being defensive and saying "You're only trying to...," you are politely acknowledging, "Yes, I know you want the kids to do well." Or, "I can understand your desire for peace and quiet." Or whatever the goal may be.

2. *I see why this goal is so important to you because*_____
   _____. This disarming statement is so important. It helps undo any threat from the past that may bring up fears of abandonment or other terrifying possibilities.

3. *I appreciate you for your efforts and character, for example,*
   _____. Almost any expression of appreciation or affirmation will do. Don't proceed until you have expressed a positive attitude.

4. *I have the same goal and have worked toward it by*
   _____. If appropriate or necessary, this is your opportunity to apologize and begin making amends if you have disappointed or hurt the other person. Making amends will help restore trust, so the other will eventually be more open to your appeal.

5. *I'm concerned that our current method might not accomplish this goal because* _____ .

6 *I suggest* _____ .

7. *I'd be willing to help by* _____ .

8. *What do you think?*

Try to use a story or analogy to explain the problem with the method being used so that you speak to the heart not just the head. Sometimes the method that people employ to accomplish a particular goal might be perfectly acceptable and would work fine—*under different circumstances.*

For example, a young military officer was standing at the kitchen sink washing the dishes. His wife wanted to spontaneously express her love for him so she sneaked up behind him and put her arms around him. The soldier dropped a plate on the floor and it broke. He wheeled around, braced himself, and threw his wife halfway across the room. He stood immobilized for a moment, grimly awaiting another assault. Then he came to himself, enfolded his weeping wife in his arms, and comforted her. Needless to say, he felt very embarrassed and ashamed of himself.

This young soldier had just returned from the Vietnam War, where he had been decorated for bravery as a Green Beret. He had been trained, drilled, and hardened to respond instinctively to attack. His specialty was one-on-one combat. He was an impeccably qualified commando warrior. His wife's goal of spontaneous lovemaking was wonderful. Under the circumstances, however, her method was clearly not appropriate.

After you've worked through this eight point format, the other person may simply take your suggestion. Without any further discussion, however, the issue at hand will probably not be settled to the satisfaction of both parties. If the individual you're appealing to gives in too easily, tell the person that you appreciate his or her cooperative attitude, but ask if the suggestion could be given a bit more thought. Then bring it up again later.

On those rare occasions where you are one hundred percent

right and the other person is one hundred percent wrong, you can still lose the struggle by holding onto a bad attitude. That's an especially good time to try out this valuable technique. It can help you avoid sinful methods of achieving good goals.

One last caution: when you first try appealing, the other person may think that you're starting a fight. Nevertheless, stick with the appeal and every time they defend themselves or counterattack, bring them back to the specific subject under discussion. "I know you have good goals. I mentioned that. I know that you've been doing some wonderful things and I appreciate what you've just pointed out. Now, I'm still concerned about the approach. Do you have any suggestions?" If you keep focusing on the positives, the chances of a fight diminish dramatically.

BEING PICKY POSITIVE

American comedian Will Rogers once said, "I've never met a man I didn't like." That was obviously a choice on his part. He had probably met a lot of people that were difficult to like, but he had chosen to like them anyway. I would guess that Rogers looked for little things, qualities that others would normally take for granted, and made a point of appreciating those things in the people he encountered.

One of the most important of all the ways in which we can reach out to other people is something I call being picky positive. This is where we choose to become a steady channel through which God can show people their identity, hope, and value. That doesn't mean we should invent things to be positive about; we choose to like people even if they are totally messed up. We don't like what they do, but we still like them.

Before we hit others with a whole list of negatives, we should try to build up their self-esteem and hope. Even when we do address what it is about the person that we dislike the most, the quality that generally irritates us, we can picture what it would be like if that grating quality were yielded to Christ.

Suppose someone is stubborn. We pause and say "What would stubbornness be if it were yielded to the Lord?" Well, yielded stubbornness becomes tenacity and patience. We need men and women of God who are not wishy-washy. You could say to a stubborn person, "I appreciate the fact that once you make up your mind, you stick with your decision. You never give up. I wish I could be more like that."

In a sense, gratitude for people's qualities—even their unpolished qualities—is a distillation of grace. Isn't that what God does for us? He says, "I choose to like you, value you, and picture your potential... just because." And he knows that the greatest gratitude, the greatest motivation comes from grace accepted not from disgrace or shame.

Grace is the most powerful of all motivators. When we extend grace to others, we find good things to say about them, while we leave the solution of their problems with God.

Sometimes we have to tell people things they don't want to hear. Sometimes we have to do things for them they don't want us to do. And sometimes we do have to keep a safe distance from certain untrustworthy people.

Let's say you're walking along with a friend and he steps into a pool of water. The water is electrified by a fallen power line. Your friend is about to be electrocuted. You realize that it won't do anyone any good for you to rush into the water and grab him. You look around frantically. Is there a fallen branch? A piece of plastic? There must be something you can use to whack the wire out of the pool. Only then will there be some hope for your friend. If you rush in and grab him you'll both die—and that doesn't help anyone.

In the same way, when we're dealing with untrustworthy, even dangerous people, we have to find a level of involvement with them that may be uncomfortable but not destructive. We will increase that involvement only as God gives us wisdom and strength.

SIN'S WINNERS AND LOSERS

When it comes to trying to help people change their behavior, bear in mind that the gap you're trying to cross is far too wide for jumping, and flapping your arms isn't going to get you across either. You have to get help from the Lord and from the body of Christ. And grace plays an absolutely crucial role in all of this.

God will give you the grace to set limits on people, to tell them things they don't want to hear, to back off, and to bring consequences to bear. At the same time he will teach you how to be encouraging and constructive and involved. He will enable you to walk through the consequences of their behavior right alongside of them. Grace will help you wait on God's timing for results.

To help us to understand this question of balance in reaching out to influence others, picture a pair of pliers.

1. I must first look at myself, and remember that grace cannot be affected by the outcome.
2. What holds this tool together is my seeking the other person's welfare.
3. One handle is investing pleasantly in the person's life.
4. The other handle is investing painfully.
5. Finally, I must leave the pressure and the results to God.

Sometimes we have to bring higher human authority to bear on other people. We have appealed to them, we have modeled for them, we have been positive, we've tried all these various approaches and nothing has changed. Sometimes we have to go over their heads, perhaps even so far as sending someone to jail for his or her own welfare. It may be the only thing that can turn that person around.

The difference between godly assertiveness and that of the secular world is simply this: from the purely secular perspective we say, "Hey, I'm somebody, too! I have my rights! I'm not going to trample on their rights, but I am going to defend my own." Now in a political or legal battle, this may be right and necessary for everyone's sake. In a free society, citizens are granted certain rights under the law which should be defended.

But we are discussing personal relationships here. In godly assertiveness we do not insist on our rights. How can we—the chief of sinners, the one who had the beam in the eye, the servant forgiven the unpayable debt—do anything based on "our rights"? We cast our basic rights as human beings upon the mercy of God, while we continue to set clear and intelligent limits for the welfare of others and ourselves. We must believe that our true reward is from the Lord and trust him to meet our needs.

Let's consider an example from God's Word about this kind of limit-setting. As an authority figure who attempted to deal with the church in Corinth, Paul knew that the people there were notorious for sexual imbalances and perversions. In short, Corinth was a city that worshiped sex. And in the church something was going on that was especially offensive: a man was having sex with his father's wife.

Paul said, "Look, you don't even have to be a Christian to know that what he's doing is wrong. The heathens don't even talk about such things. Throw him out of the church and turn him over to Satan to make him miserable" (see 1 Cor 5:5). It was Paul's hope that such severe consequences would lead the man to repentance.

In 2 Corinthians, Paul seems to be talking about the same man "It was hard for me to write that other letter. I wept over it. But I'm glad I did it because you repented! You were running around, acting proud and pretending 'Things like that don't happen in our church.' But you took my advice, and now I hear that the man that you set limits on has repented too. Why don't you take him back in?" (see 2 Cor 2:3-11).

Sometimes the absolutely best thing we can do for someone is to set limits—if we are in an appropriate relationship to do so. Certainly it is hard and costly, but "Faithful are the wounds of a friend" (Prv 27:6). In fact, most people shrink back from loving with this kind of "tough love."

Some individuals do try to use heavy control to manage the difficult people in their lives. Others, going to the opposite extreme, assume that they're never supposed to set any limits at all. We need to achieve a balance in this regard, and the balance comes from realizing that God is the one who changes hearts.

But let's consider one more question. When someone sins and that sin personally affects us, who has been most sinned against? Who is the victim? Does anyone stand to be benefited?

As we already mentioned in our discussion of the prodigal son, the one sinned against is God. David clearly stated this truth in Psalm 51:4, "Against you, you only, have I sinned."

We may grasp this concept of sin against God, but it can still be difficult not to play the victim role. Giving it up seems like such an unreasonable concept! Sometimes we certainly feel victimized. We may feel pain and loss. But we will only suffer serious damage when we choose to sin, and then only by the consequences of our own sin. Many times the sinner is most damaged by his or her own sinful response.

Does this include children before the age of accountability? This is a difficult question. Clearly they can be hurt and choose to respond in unhealthy, ungodly ways. They react to the pain but can't be expected to deal with it as mature adults. Eventually, as they grow up, the Holy Spirit will work to convince them that they need help.

At this point, children move into the age of accountability. It is only after they see their need for grace and refuse it, that they accrue permanent damage. If they acknowledge their need and accept help, they will still struggle with their scars and unbalanced patterns, but God will immediately start to bring glory from the struggle. Eventually they will agree with Joseph that those who hurt them meant it for evil but God meant it for good.

We benefit from the sin. You see, strange as it sounds, even though someone else's sin can seriously affect us, we can be spared victimization. If we walk through the consequences of someone else's sin with God, wc will actually end up benefiting as a result. This wonderful truth radically portrays God's unending creativity of redemption—taking the very worst someone can throw at us and turning it into gold in our own lives if we turn it over to him.

GLORIOUS TRIALS

The best example of this principle can be seen in Jesus hanging on the cross. Jesus was totally innocent of wrongdoing, but he did not endure the crucifixion moaning and groaning about the severity of his victimization. He threw himself and his enemies into the merciful hands of God. Because of this supreme sacrifice of his own life for our sake, we can today say, "Thank God for the cross." When we look upon the cross of Jesus Christ, we now see an object of ultimate beauty and glory because of God's redemptive act in giving his own Son to be killed at the hands of the human race.

When people hurt you, you really can rejoice and be exceedingly glad because it is in these very struggles that you are given the opportunity to bring glory to God. As you respond to the trial in a godly way, God is bringing glory to you. In your pain, you lay up treasure in heaven. The world is full of pain. Remember, when it comes, that suffering is the substance from which God produces true freedom.

"My brethren, count it all joy," James wrote, "when you fall into various trials, knowing that the testing of your faith produces patience. But let patience have its perfect work, that you may be perfect and complete, lacking nothing" (Jas 1:2-4).

As we apply God's truth to our daily lives, we learn how to give up our own attempts to grasp value, power, and hope. And as we allow God's grace to provide us with those qualities, we will be able to draw a line that reflects the mercy of God. As we move into true freedom, our bitterness will vanish and gratitude will take its place. The profound belief that God loves us compels us to act in love for God, others, and self.

A spirit of true gratitude is a gift from God. Because this question of gratitude is such a difficult one for hurting humans to embrace, I would like to address this topic in greater detail in the next chapter. If only we could learn to truly thank God in all circumstances, how different our lives would be.

8 | Gratitude: The Great Motivator

G ERALDINE NERVOUSLY SHOVED a lock of gray-streaked hair out of her eyes and shook her head in frustration. "I don't see what there is to be thankful for, Dr. Bell. Let's be realistic."

She and I were discussing gratitude because of Geraldine's constant struggle with anxiety. She worried constantly. Then Geraldine would feel guilty about being anxious, since she knew that Christians were not supposed to be anxious. This cycle of worry and guilt was very difficult for her to overcome.

I tried to clarify my point. "I don't think it's unrealistic for you to thank God for the anxious feelings you're having. That's what he wants you to do."

"What do you mean, thank him? Thank him for disobeying him by being worried? I can understand being grateful for blessings and things like that. But I think it's crazy to thank God for having inappropriate feelings."

Still a bit annoyed, Geraldine mulled over our conversation as she drove to the hospital where her mother-in-law lay dying in the intensive care unit. Vast waves of anxiety suddenly overwhelmed this woman as she sat in the ICU waiting room. Our conversation came to mind again, prompting a reluctant prayer: "OK, God. Thank you for the anxiety."

The Lord responded to her immediately. "You're going to have to decide who you fear the most—me or your in-laws."

All at once Geraldine realized that her anxiety centered around God's desire for her to share God's way of salvation with the dying woman in the next room. It wasn't going to be a popular thing to do as far as the family was concerned. Her husband's brothers and sisters barely tolerated Christianity.

Geraldine tightened up her resolve. *I'm going to fear God and no one else,* she told herself.

Walking into the sick woman's room and seeing her own rebellious teenage daughter standing there did not at all alleviate her nervousness—quite the opposite, as you can imagine. Kathy was the last person she wanted in the room when she shared the gospel with Grandma. But Geraldine was determined that she would fear God, and God alone. Not her in-laws. Not even her sarcastic, critical daughter.

Geraldine quietly spoke to her mother-in-law, tenderly holding her hand. The elderly woman, knowing she faced death, finally grasped her need for the good news of eternal life and gladly agreed to receive Christ as her Savior. Just as Geraldine began to pray with her, she felt an arm encircle her waist. Her daughter had been listening to the gentle words her mother had spoken. With tears in her eyes, Kathy embraced her mother.

"I want to tell you something, Mom. I want to be right with Jesus, too."

Geraldine learned a valuable lesson that day. God has a way of turning the most unpleasant things in our lives into blessings—if we're willing to be grateful for them. Our gratitude serves as a statement of faith that God will, indeed, work all things together for good.

Some friends of ours also experienced a hospital encounter which brought similar results. Pastor Vern Kline and his wife Patty were driving to a revival meeting and happily chatting about the opportunity to share about the Lord in a new town. Just then a shriek of brakes and an enormous crash left them showered with broken glass and smeared with blood.

The next thing Vern and Patty knew, they were in the trauma center at a local hospital being treated for their injuries. Vern rested his head on his freshly-stitched hand. "Why?" he kept asking himself. "Why? WHY?" Why such a senseless accident when he and Patty had been so excited about the revival?

Suddenly God's voice broke through into Vern's mind. "Don't ask why. Just thank me! I know what I'm doing."

In spite of his disappointment and pain, Vern wanted most of all to obey God. "Thanks, Lord. Thank you for your intentions in this."

Neither Vern nor Patty had been badly injured in the accident. After being stitched up and treated for abrasions, they were about to leave the hospital when the attending physician rushed over to where they were. His face was grave.

"Could I talk to both of you for just a moment?" he asked. "I want to show you something." Vern and Patty sat down with the doctor and listened.

"I'm concerned about some irregular findings on a routine X-ray," he began. He held up the transparency to the light and pointed to an unevenly shaped area. "Mrs. Kline, you have a mass in your abdomen that needs to be evaluated." Patty and Vern looked at each other in shock. They made an appointment with their physician the following morning.

Within days, a biopsy confirmed that Patty had cancer. However, the doctors were able to treat this malignancy since it was in a very early stage. And because it was arrested in time, the cancerous cells had not yet metastasized. Years have passed since her surgery and Patty's cancer has not recurred.

Vern still smiles when he tells the story. "God saved Patty's life by allowing that accident to happen. But what amazes me is that he instructed me to thank him—before I understood why. God is so wise, and so amazingly sovereign."

Sometimes the Lord brings us to understand his intentions. Sometimes we never find out. But he has called us to rejoice in everything, regardless of our own ability to figure things out. And we confirm our trust in God every time we do so.

At face value, God's call for gratitude seems a little extreme. When does he want us to be grateful? Always. For what? Everything. That doesn't leave much room for whining and grumbling, does it?

GROWING UP WITH GREAT EXPECTATIONS

During the first several months of infancy, we human beings consider ourselves to be the center of the universe. Unless we have been born into an abusive family or into some other circumstance that results in a lack of nurture, we believe that everything will usually go our way. All we have to do is scream a little bit and all those big people come running over to meet our needs.

Then we begin to discover a scary truth. Those big people don't have to take care of us, and when they do, it's not always according to our own timetable. As a matter of fact, wise parents begin to introduce an ideal level of frustration. Without making the baby feel desperate and miserable, parents don't rush to meet the child's needs too quickly, either. Some balance must be maintained or a spoiled brat begins to emerge.

At this point, we humans begin to create a crucial concept known as *rights* in our tiny, developing minds. We conceive of these rights as things that we expect and which, in our childlike way, we demand. If our desires aren't immediately met, we communicate our disapproval. We may do this by staging a horrible tantrum. When we're one or two years old, this method generally works pretty well. Somebody rushes over to solve the problem. Many of us quickly learn that somebody usually "fixes" our frustration if we stir up enough of an emotional storm.

This sort of behavior is to be expected from toddlers. But unfortunately, whether we resort to histrionics or other equally inappropriate measures, some of us carry these expectations all the way into adulthood.

Take the example of Stan, who had been pampered by his doting mother. She did everything for him and always rushed in to fix the problems he created for himself. This spoiled, undisciplined man had then married a non-confrontational wife, Bonnie, who had continued the inordinate coddling practiced by her mother-in-law.

By the age of thirty, Stan was a heavy-drinking alcoholic, irresponsible, barely able to earn a living, and occasionally violent.

Bonnie had patiently put up with his drinking for years, not knowing what else to do. But when she began to search for answers as the situation worsened, Bonnie received good counsel from members of her church about how she had actually been supporting Stan's alcoholism. Once she learned the truth about her own unhealthy behavior, this wife realized that she couldn't cover for her husband any longer.

Bonnie told me later that confronting Stan was the hardest thing she had ever done. It was harder than covering up for him. It was harder than cleaning up after him. It was even harder than being bruised and battered by him. But one day Bonnie found the courage to say, "Stan, you're going to have to move out of the house. I need you to stay somewhere else. You've also got to get yourself into therapy. We can't go on like this."

Bonnie had done what she had to do, but the worst was yet to come. Stan moved out, but his behavior became even more out of control. Sometimes he came by the house drunk, ranting and raving, threatening the lives of his wife and three sons. As his drinking problem accelerated, there appeared to be no hope for change.

One day when Bonnie was driving to work, she saw her husband, the father of her boys, lying in the gutter beside the road. She drove around the block four times, pondering what she should do, not even knowing for sure if Stan was dead or alive. Bonnie knew only one thing for sure. She knew that if she pulled Stan out of the gutter she would be reinforcing the lie that he had believed all his life. This grown man really thought that he didn't have to do his part. He could make a mess of everything, and somebody else would always fix it for him.

Sick at heart, with tears streaming down her face, Bonnie drove on to work, leaving Stan behind her in the gutter. All she could do was pray and wait and wonder. That took a tremendous amount of courage.

A little later in the day, Stan regained consciousness. Gradually, after reaching that all-time low, he realized that he might have died lying there beside the road. For the first time in his life, he realized that no one was going to rescue him. At long last, Stan went for help. Little by little, he mended his life with the

Lord's help. Eventually, the marriage was brought back together again.

Until he came to the end of his rope, Stan had thought he had the "right" to be rescued, fixed, and cleaned up. In our own minds we usually create a long list of our own "rights" or needs. When these often unverbalized needs are met, we take them for granted. When they aren't, we usually become angry. Many items on our list emanate directly out of our family backgrounds.

If, for example, I grew up in a home where three square meals a day appeared without much work on my part, I would probably think that the world owes me three square meals a day. Or consider a boy who grew up in a home where Mom held a full time job, but still managed to do the dishes and laundry and spoil the kids. When he gets married, he'll probably think that's what a wife is supposed to do.

Of course, we may very well turn around and grant certain rights to other people. But it's usually a far shorter list since we can't possibly be as aware of someone else's needs as we are of our own. So one person puts together one list of rights, and then marries someone who mentally carries around an entirely different list. These two people are going to step on each other's toes. It's unavoidable. The same phenomenon can happen on a less intimate level when people come together in a friendship, in a business relationship, or in a service role at church.

Then the devil comes along and says "If they truly loved you, if they were really caring, they would simply *know* what you need." We seem to believe that our rights are self-evident, that they are perfectly obvious—even when they are far from crystal-clear in our own minds. People step on one of them without even trying and then we feel angry at the slight. Over a period of time, that anger piles up and eventually turns into bitterness.

As Christians we come to realize that we actually have *no* rights. We are former inmates of "death row" who have been pardoned, cleansed, justified, and adopted by the very God we've offended. What we really deserve is eternal separation from God. What makes us think we have the right to *demand* from God or others—as if we were still the center of our very own little universe?

LEARNING TO BE GRATEFUL

God wants us to choose to be grateful for every little thing. We say, "I can't do it! How can I be grateful for *everything*—especially when the pain of life sometimes seems so overwhelming?" One woman recently told me about an incident that occurred while her son was dying of cancer. Someone from her church had admonished her, with a patronizing pat on the arm, "Now, now, dear. All things work together for good. We're supposed to be grateful."

When this woman came in to see me she told me she had wanted to choke this bearer of seemingly pious platitudes. "Wait until *your* son is dying of cancer," the heartsick woman spat out. "Then see if *you* are able to walk that path!"

Although her friend was trying to communicate a valid principle, she picked the wrong time. The distraught mother was in too much pain to grasp the principle of gratitude. We can find it impossible to feel grateful, especially when we're already stretched to the breaking point.

I have found it helpful to know that I don't have to *feel* grateful to state gratitude. It also helps to know that I'm always free to fight against sin and carelessness if someone meant an attack for evil. God hates the sin and wants the sinner to repent. Nevertheless we have a God so big that he can allow evil and mean it for good (Gn 50:20).

I have seen profound freedom come to people heavily burdened by bitterness when they come to the point of saying thank you for it all. What happens if we refuse to give thanks? We keep checking and measuring to see if God has brought enough good from the evil for us to let go of our victim mentality. Instead we should live like Fannie Crosby who was blinded by the mistake of a quack doctor as a baby. She went on to become one of the greatest hymn writers of all time. In her later years Fannie stated that if she had her life to live all over again, she would want to be blind again. I call that true freedom. She rose above the victim role to the role of victor.

Can we learn to be grateful for the bad things as well as the good? Each time we get angry or irritated, let's pause and say,

"Thank you, Lord. I'm grateful for everything you allow into my life. Teach me not to fear discomfort. Teach me to not fear dysfunction. Teach me not to fear what people can do to me. Instead, help me to fear my own sin." God has promised us that no test we'll ever go through or any pain is so great that we will have to sin.

I suggest that you begin by practicing gratitude very mechanically. To begin with, you might set yourself the goal of saying one positive thing to each member of your family each day. You could buy some thank-you notes and plan on writing at least two of them a week. Rehearse watching the people around you, looking for things about which you can be positive. Remember our discussion of being picky positive in the last chapter?

I try to practice this principle in my own life. In fact, I've taken the time to write down a lot of the things for which I am grateful. Sometimes when I feel overwhelmed with irritants, I pause and mentally review my list. Then I realize that the good things in my life far outweigh my problems. I'm trying to learn to be grateful not only for what makes me happy but also for what irritates me as well. Like Geraldine, we often make the mistake of thanking God only for what we consider to be blessings.

Consider the oft-used example of a church group driving somewhere in snowy weather. The driver loses control, the vehicle slides on the ice and smashes into a tree. The car is totalled, a couple of passengers suffer broken legs, the driver gets whiplash, but nobody gets killed.

Next Sunday one of them gives this testimony at church, "I'd just like to thank the Lord that nobody was killed in the accident last weekend."

We should certainly be grateful for that fact, but I believe that God's expectation for gratitude far surpasses the obvious. We aren't supposed to simply thank the Lord that it could have been worse. I believe we are to thank the Lord for the accident itself, for the broken legs, for the whiplash, and for the totalled car. It is especially in those very unpleasant and difficult circumstances that we grow and develop character.

Naturally, this kind of total gratitude goes against our grain. Corrie ten Boom told many stories about the years she spent in a Nazi concentration camp. Out of all the abominable conditions, one thing that bothered the female prisoners most was the lice that gnawed at them all the time. The women itched, tossing and turning, night and day because of these tiny creatures. To add to their misery and humiliation, the women had to have their heads shaved.

While they were having devotions in the barracks, one of the Christian women suddenly said, "I think we should thank God for the lice."

"What do you mean? There's nothing good about lice! Why, you can't even eat them!"

Try as they might, these women couldn't find a single reason, but they decided to express their gratitude to God for the lice anyway. It wasn't many days before a prisoner from another area said to them, "You know, you ought to be grateful for those lice of yours."

"What!?" These Christian women were all ears. "Why should we be grateful?"

As they listened to this prisoner's explanation, tears stung their eyes. The lice kept the guards out of their barracks. The lice secured for them freedom to express their faith to one another, freedom to care for each other, and freedom from even worse abuse. Those wretched insects had in effect created a safe haven for these women, virtually insulating them in the lice-infested barracks from the horrible mistreatment and indignity that was occurring all around them in the camp.

What if you yourself had suffered as a prisoner in the Nazi concentration camps? What if a careless driver totalled your brand new car? What if an enemy deliberately sabotaged the car to cause you personal injury? Perhaps hardest of all, what if a friend turned on you and sued you for all you had? When Ephesians 5:20 exhorts us to be grateful for all things, I believe it means *all things.*

Ingratitude is a sinful pattern that can lead to severe emotional damage. On the other hand, gratitude is a powerful motivator, especially in calling us on to obey God. Gratitude teaches us to see the world through different eyes—not by way of rose-colored spectacles but by confirming and authenticating our faith.

So what holds us back? *We are afraid.* If we thank God for our difficulties, maybe he won't fix them, or maybe we won't be motivated to try fixing ourselves. We fear that if we express gratitude, people will never change. They'll think that we don't care about the problems they cause. The truth is that when we are grateful, people become much more motivated to examine themselves and change. And we ourselves seem to find a new spring in our step.

STEPPING INTO FAITH

What is faith? Most Christians answer that question with a familiar quote from Paul's faith-focused letter to the Hebrews, "Now faith is the substance of things hoped for, the evidence of things not seen" (Heb 11:1). And, of course, that's a good answer. When we have faith, it does give substance to our hope and makes that hope stronger.

I believe that having faith amounts to *obeying God.* As we do what God asks us to do, we are able to overcome all sorts of sin and weakness through the power of faith. As we believe that God loves us, we are able to endure the discomforts of obedience. Having faith requires six elements within us:

1. *To express faith we need motivation.* We are motivated toward faith by two things: gratitude for what God has done and hope in what he is going to do. Scripture says "he who comes to God must believe that He is, and that He is the rewarder of those who diligently seek Him" (Heb 11:6). We have to believe that if we act in faith, we will be rewarded. We may be a little surprised when that reward actually comes, but we have nonetheless somehow held tightly to our belief that God will come through. Hope and gratitude drive us to obey.

2. *To express faith we need a specific principle to obey.* To act in faith, we act upon a principle of life such as walking the second mile, turning the other cheek, praying without

ceasing, or some other similar guideline. We obey in faith because we believe that if we act in accordance with that principle, God will bring his power into the surrounding circumstances. Our obedience doesn't *fix* anything, but it gives God something to work with.

3. *To express faith, we need a situation in which that principle applies.* When our circumstances cause us some sort of discomfort, we search for solutions. We then come to understand our powerlessness and seek God's help. Our difficult circumstances have driven us to seek hope and to find an appropriate principle or promise. This pursuit amounts to obeying, in faith, God's will for us.

4. *To express faith, we may need to experience an uncomfortable reaction at the thought of obeying.* Sometimes obedience costs us. We might say, "I can't, it's too hard." "I'll look like a fool." "Not now." "My heart isn't in it, so it won't count." In faith, we have to overcome the obstacles to obedience.

5. *To express faith, we need to obey regardless of how we feel about it.*

6. *To express faith, we need to rest in God's grace before, during, and after obedience, knowing that our feeble efforts count and the results are God's.*

What are the things that we can't do? When we exercise faith we integrate our hope with a biblical principle in a difficult situation. That's all we're required to do. The rest is God's responsibility. There are some things that we *don't* have to worry about. God's job is to:

- declare us worthy
- generate motivation
- take care of results
- pick the perfect time, place, and method
- help us understand why
- give us strength and stamina

God usually does not work on our timetable. To us, he either seems too fast or too slow. But if we didn't have to wait for God, we would never have to use faith. Romans 8:24-25 says, "For we were saved in this hope, but hope that is seen is not hope; for why does one still hope for what he sees? But if we hope for what we do not see then we eagerly wait for it with perseverance."

If we didn't care about the results, we wouldn't be exercising faith in the first place. We have been programmed to focus on results. But *results* are God's business; *obedience* is our business. God knows what he is doing. He knows so many things we don't. God's ways really are so far above our ways as to belong to a different realm.

A pastor friend of mine especially enjoyed witnessing and passing out tracts. As he went into the neighborhood supermarket one night, the Lord said, "See that man on the telephone over there? I want you to give him a tract."

The pastor reacted negatively, muttering to himself, "That's crazy. It would seem like I'm afraid to talk to him directly. I'll wait till he gets off the phone."

The Lord said, "Don't give me all this trouble. Just give him a tract."

The pastor figured it couldn't hurt anything, so he handed the man a tract and went about his business in the grocery store. A few minutes later, the man who had been talking on the telephone came rushing up to him. "Are you a pastor?" he asked breathlessly.

"Yes, as a matter of fact, I am."

He said, "When you came up to me, I was talking to a friend about Jesus. We were talking about some questions I have and my friend couldn't answer them. Could we talk?"

Of course, the pastor gladly took the man out to his car and led him to the Lord. The Lord knows how to get results. When he indicates that he wants us to do something, it's not our job to pick the perfect time, place, or method.

We sometimes try to avoid obedience by saying, "God couldn't use someone as bad off as I am." Most of us have hidden some pretty ugly skeletons in the back of the closet—things we've done, things we haven't done, maybe even things that have been done to us. These skeletons make us feel worthless. We also often use them as an excuse not to obey. We are right to feel unworthy in the presence of God. But as we become aware of our unworthiness, we need to allow God to make us worthy through his infinite grace.

When we act in faith, we are being obedient to God whether we feel like it or not. What if you ask your children to clean their room and they say, "No! I don't want to!"?

How do you respond? "Oh! I'm sorry, I didn't realize you didn't want to. Well, that's fine. You go ahead and play. I'll do it." You had better not respond that way, or you'll do your kids a lot of harm. A wise parent would say, "I didn't ask you if you *wanted* to; I told you to obey. Here are the consequences if you do. Here are the consequences if you don't."

I find it helpful to remember that my reluctance and fear are nothing compared to what Christ suffered when he obeyed his Father and went to the cross. What if Jesus had lost heart in the midst of his trial and said, "I don't feel like it anymore"? Jesus himself learned obedience through what he suffered (Heb 5:8). He didn't arrive at the foot of the cross fresh from a trouble-free jaunt through life as a pampered prince. If he had, he surely would have turned back.

Sometimes we react to faith situations by saying, "It just doesn't make any sense. It seems unfair. Why me?" I hear this so frequently in my practice. People are always complaining about unfairness. I ask them, "would you really like to be treated fairly?"

"Sure," they respond.

"OK," I say, "let's pray and ask God to give you right now exactly what you deserve."

"Wait, wait," they cry out, "I see your point. Life is both unfairly hard and unfairly merciful." They quit whining about fairness.

It's also not our job to generate sufficient strength and stamina. Do you ever hear yourself sort of whining, "I can't... I'm just too weak. It's just too hard. I'd never be able to keep it up if I did it." Strength and stamina come to us from God, not from ourselves.

Our responsibility is to try right now—in this very moment—

to yield ourselves to obedience. That feeling of weakness serves to remind us that, yes, we are indeed powerless. But God's power at work in us will prove more than enough to get the job done.

> *Lord, I have obeyed. Thank you for helping me to obey.*
> *The results are your responsibility.*
> *My trying is valuable no matter what the results.*
> *My efforts, feeble though they are, are in your hands.*
> *I know that you will use them for your glory.*
> *Thank you for your continued grace to trust you.*

WEAPONS OF FAITH

As I have said throughout this book, God's grace gives us value, power, and hope. Since the devil can't diminish the grace we have been given, he attacks our awareness of these three important benefits of grace. Satan continually tries to make us feel worthless, helpless, and hopeless. We have already covered three basic weapons for fighting back and for calming ourselves down in order to keep the channels of grace flowing freely.

1. When we are feeling overwhelmed, we acknowledge that things are hard for us. We are weak. We admit, "I can't generate value, be strong, or secure my future."

2. We don't fight back on that point, and we don't try to be stronger. In fact, we want to get weaker so God can be stronger through us. We claim, "But God can..."

3. Then we affirm that God can and wants to and will. And so we decide, *"I will try with confidence and rest in God for results, so here goes..."*

I want you to see some of the ways in which you can practice becoming more aware of your own level of freedom in these areas. It's easy enough to say, "I'm powerless." But watch yourself as the day goes along. You may notice yourself trying to make things go right, driven by "I must" and "I should."

Maybe I could give you an example to help you comprehend your awareness of powerlessness. Let's say that I'm in Chicago, walking in the park along Lake Shore Drive. I notice that a man is standing on the edge of Lake Michigan. The poor fellow is jumping up and down and flapping his arms. He looks very tired. Being a compassionate person I walk over and say, "Sir, what are you doing?"

"Oh," he says, "I have to fly across Lake Michigan. I absolutely have to fly across Lake Michigan."

I shake my head kindly and assure him, "Sir, there is no way you can fly by flapping your arms and jumping up and down like that."

"I was beginning to suspect that," he nods wearily. "But, you see, I *have* to. I'm going to keep trying because I have to fly across Lake Michigan."

I ask, "Have you ever heard of airports and airplanes?"

"No," he answers, trying to flap and talk at the same time. "Tell me about them."

"Well if you'll stop jumping and flapping for a moment, I'll explain. Look up in the sky. You see all those airplanes flying over your head?"

"Ah, yes. I wondered what they were. They seemed awfully big and noisy to be birds."

"You're right, they aren't birds. People ride in them. If you go over there to O'Hare Airport, buy a ticket, and get on a plane, it won't be long before you'll be flying across Lake Michigan."

This exhausted man feels deeply relieved. He can now stop flapping his arms and jumping and trying because he has an alternative way to accomplish his goal. But he seemed unable to admit his powerlessness until he had been presented with a viable solution.

I once asked a young patient who kept forgetting his true powerlessness to climb up on a chair, flap his arms, and jump each time he realized he was feeling as if he should be strong. This man felt silly, but not half as silly as he should have felt for trying to be strong without God's grace. We have to get it through our heads that we really are powerless. Rather than becoming stronger, we need to become weaker and get out of God's way so he can live strongly through us.

We want to yield ourselves completely to God, but what do we really do? We run around saying, "Yes, yes, that's what God says but that is for saints, for strong people. It doesn't work in the real world." God wants us to quit procrastinating and at least begin wherever we can to yield ourselves to his grace.

IDENTIFYING POINTS OF WEAKNESS

What kinds of behavioral patterns do you see in your own life which continually frustrate you? I would suggest that you pick one unhealthy pattern in particular and try to boil it down to one or two sentences. A pattern exhibits three parts: a situation, how we respond to it, and the result of our behavior.

Here are a few examples to serve as guidelines, but be sure to write out your own pattern in your own words. Sinful behavioral patterns are very individualized, even though we can often see some common denominators.

- When I'm emotionally overwhelmed, I drink and my drinking disrupts my family.
- When I get my feelings hurt, I sulk or isolate myself until I feel better, and the offense never gets resolved.
- When I want to control people, I try to be super-nice and generous, but I always end up feeling used and exploited.
- When my children don't obey me, I lose my temper and verbally abuse them. This damages them and makes me hate myself.
- When my husband ignores me or speaks to me unkindly, I find myself flirting with other men. Sometimes this leads to sexual encounters. I wind up hating myself, my husband, and God.
- When my parents come to visit, I feel I have to have every meal planned ahead, everything perfect. I become irritable and frustrated. To make matters worse, they never give me their approval, which makes me resentful.

- When I'm at work, I don't like having anyone looking over my shoulder telling me what to do, so I get defensive about supervision. Since this causes problems with my bosses, I've lost a couple of jobs over my insubordination.

With these examples in mind, think about the behavioral patterns you would most like to overcome. What would you like to stop, or even start, doing? Ask God to reveal to you one particular area in which you need to change, then listen carefully for his guidance. Remember that you can't take on too much at once. You can't manage to overhaul your whole life in one fell swoop, even with the help of God's grace.

Keep track of these tendencies. The next step is to keep a log of how often this pattern hits you. Before you start trying to work on it, first try to become more aware of just how pervasive it really is. Sometimes we say, "Yeah, I guess I do have that problem but it's not all that bad. I'm sure it doesn't cause me trouble very often." It's helpful to acknowledge how very often certain patterns do exert a powerful effect on us.

"I can't fix this myself." Now we have to make a painful admission. Not only are we so messed up that we can't quit, but part of us doesn't even want to. We don't really hate our sin; we hate the consequences of the sin. If we could find some way to indulge in our sin and not suffer any consequences, we would probably go right back to it. That's why we have to admit the awful truth to God: "First, I ask you to help me, and then when you try, I actively block your grace."

Once I told one of my patients, "You not only can't change, but there's a part of you that doesn't even want to." This woman got so mad she threw her hat at me! Fortunately, it was a nice soft fur hat so it didn't hurt. She was offended because she wanted to claim that although she was too weak to change, at least she could take credit for wanting to.

So there's part of us that knows we need to change and a part that doesn't want to even acknowledge the gravity of the problem. No matter. Just thank God that, in spite of our confusion, he floods us with his infinite grace. In fact, that's what humility really means—accepting that God's grace applies to me despite my own mess.

After we admit *"I can't,"* then we can take that giant step in faith and say, *"But God can."* Having taken a good look at our powerlessness, we remember that God not only can change us, he really wants to. So we say, "God has the power and I need to let go and let him do his part."

STILL NO RESULTS IN SIGHT?

It's OK to say "Let go and let God," but be sure when you say it, that you know exactly what it is you're releasing to him. And don't expect to see instant results. Results are often foremost in our minds, yet God usually asks us to obey before he gives us any results.

As a dynamic missionary in China, I'm sure that Hudson Taylor couldn't always see the fruit of his labor, but he had to trust in God for every one of the millions of Chinese Christians now in heaven due to his visionary work. On one occasion, Taylor was on his way out to China on a sailing vessel when the ship ran into trouble. With no wind whatsoever to move the boat, they were steadily drifting toward a dangerous reef and an island which was inhabited by cannibals. The crew hurriedly tried to drop the anchor and wait for a change in the weather, but somehow the anchor got all fouled up and wouldn't go down. All those aboard that ship were in imminent danger.

For some reason, the captain remembered this missionary passenger who could pray. So he rushed below and filled Taylor in on the situation, pleading with him to intercede on their behalf. The man of faith searched the captain's face. "Well, I'll make you a deal. You go up and tell your men to raise the sail even though there is no wind, no clouds, and no sign of change. And I will pray."

The captain complained a little bit but he figured he had little choice. Reluctantly, he agreed. Feeling rather foolish, he went up to the deck and ordered the men to raise the sail. It seemed like a ridiculous thing to do but they did it anyway.

Taylor began to pray. Before long, a little breeze came out of nowhere and started to whip at the sail. The breeze grew stronger. Pretty soon a small cloud came over the horizon and began to grow larger and blacker. The wind stiffened and swiftly blew them away from the island. The waves grew more turbulent; a gale began to howl. Frantically, the crew began to take the sails back down.

Suddenly the captain remembered. He raced downstairs and shouted, "Mr. Taylor, you'd better stop praying. There is a storm out there!"

I think God has a wry sense of humor. Very often he asks us to step out and try when it makes no sense to our human understanding. Afterward we may well understand why. But at the outset, we can only cling to God, who asks us to believe that he is sufficient, even in the face of huge obstacles.

After we have admitted how powerless we are and declared our faith in God's power, step three is doing our part. It's sort of a *"Here goes..."* approach, as we step out in faith and hope for the best. We often have trouble moving ahead because we're waiting until we have it all perfectly figured out first as a way to alleviate anxiety.

CAUGHT UP IN THE WAVES OF ENTHUSIASM

We have seen how humility leads us out of our pride and helps us to overcome our unhealthy behavior patterns. We begin to replace our greed or drivenness with fear of the Lord. We learn to overcome our bitterness with gratitude. If this radical transformation proceeds according to plan, we will find ourselves with a new emotion—something that can surge into our spirits, replacing our sensual cravings. What is this very rare emotion which feels almost like a new drive? *Enthusiasm.*

Imagine how a race horse feels as he awaits the signal to run. The horse isn't concerned about the stress of the race—in fact, that's what it lives for. He can't wait to burst out of the holding gate. Or try to envision how a hunting dog feels when let out of the kennel for a hunt. The dog tugs against the harness, straining to run free. Or to put this concept on a more human level, think about how a craftsman feels when presented with a task which he finds challenging and stimulating. If he knows he can do it well, he can't wait to start.

This is the kind of emotion we begin to experience as we grow in grace. Enthusiasm is one of the astounding rewards awaiting those who cross the line and obey God. Of course, our motivation increases a little when we understand that we really don't have any other options. Do you remember how Simon Peter replied when Jesus asked if the disciples wished to abandon him along with all the others? "Lord, to whom shall we go? You have the words of eternal life. And we believe and are sure that You are the Christ, the Son of the living God" (Jn 6:68-69). I believe that the "grain of mustard seed" faith is knowing God is our only hope—nothing else will work.

Enthusiasm could be described as gratitude carried to the extreme. It comes from the awareness that God *cannot* fail us, that he *cannot* break his promises, that he is committed to bringing good out of bad. With enthusiasm, we can say, "Yes! I wholeheartedly accept your offer of value, power, hope. And I can't wait to see what you're going to do with me!"

Doesn't this sound glorious? It is, but not without price. We must first get into the trenches and fight. Following Christ sometimes involves grisly warfare, primarily hand-to-hand combat against ourselves. How can you enter into this kind of warfare with enough knowledge not to shoot yourself in the foot? Let's go on in the next chapter to learn more about this crucial subject.

CHAPTER 9 | Rebuilding the Walls

T HE BOOK OF NEHEMIAH in the Old Testament recounts an amazing story. Having taken on the project of rebuilding the broken down walls of ancient Jerusalem, the Israelites accomplished this huge undertaking against incredible odds. Strong political powers were arrayed against them. Local residents mocked them and threatened them. The Hebrews were few in number, and surrounded by enemies. But undaunted, they kept their eyes on their goal, trusted the God of Israel, and saw their labors through to the end.

As they worked, the message came down the line that their enemies planned to attack. But the rebuilding efforts never ceased. The workers simply kept weapons of warfare right alongside their collection of construction tools. An arsenal of spears and swords was added to the hammers, trowels, and plumblines. Whenever danger loomed, the Israelites sounded a trumpet and swiftly came to one another's aid.

God's courageous people were committed to their mission. They had a will to work. And because of their faith, their diligence, and their skill, the Israelites accomplished their objective. Soon the rubble of the past was turned into a well-constructed, protective wall.

This story of remarkable courage and dedication provides a biblical model for the work Christian believers face in two areas: warfare and reconstruction. All of us live broken lives to some degree. Not only do we have to clear away the rubble from the past but we also have to use some of it as structural material for rebuilding in the future. From Nehemiah we can learn a great deal about the task we have at hand.

What kind of warfare should we expect? For most of us, life seems challenging enough without the added dimension of going to war. I'm sure we would all rather skip this part and go on to the victory celebration.

What kind of warfare should we expect? We are warned in Scripture that we are not battling against visible, earthly warriors, but against spiritual forces: "For we do not wrestle against flesh and blood, but against principalities, against powers, against the rulers of the darkness of this age, against spiritual wickedness in the heavenly places. Therefore take up the whole armor of God, that you may be able to withstand in the evil day, and having done all, to stand" (Eph 6:12-13).

HOW DO WE PREPARE FOR THIS INVISIBLE BATTLE?

An invisible battle is raging all around us. Whether we like it or not, we are already involved. The recommendations I've made in this book are intended to break the power of the enemy in your life, to destroy his plots against you, and to defeat him in his life-and-death struggle for your heart, soul, and mind. With that in mind, let's look at ten strategic steps of warfare, some of which we have already mentioned in previous chapters.

Step number one: join the army. Accept the purpose and power your faith in Christ brings. We were automatically inducted into God's army when we became part of the body of Christ, by accepting God's grace. But many Christians have neglected their responsibilities in the warfare.

Step number two: admit your personal weakness. We have already paid a lot of attention to this element of following God into battle. Our blindness, poverty, frenzy, and helplessness are well documented by past failures and sins. We face up to our weakness when we renounce our pride.

Step number three: ask God to show you where you need to grow. We discussed how to do this in chapter eight. We need to recognize that we're not fit for war, that we have no idea where to begin. A good way to pray is this: "Lord, search my past and present and prepare me for the war, but hide from me that which I can't yet handle."

Step number four: obtain weapons and tools and the skill to use them. Christians often wander into battle equipped for a picnic in the cool shade of summertime. We feel ready to scold the enemy and throw mud at him. But are we prepared to be "more than conquerors" (Rom 8:37), able to defeat Satan and devastate his best efforts?

According to Scripture, God grants us mighty spiritual weapons for the purpose of pulling down Satan's strongholds. In the next chapter, we will list in more detail many practical tools and weapons. But even when we have the equipment we need, we remain unprepared to actually participate in a war until we've practiced how to use this equipment. We have to learn which tool performs what task. And we have to get used to using our tools and our weapons in actual combat.

Step number five: learn how to predict dangerous situations, spot ambushes, and detect signals of attack. Paul had to remind the Roman Christians that they were dead to sin and alive to God (see Rom 6). Why? Because they weren't *acting* dead to sin. They were being enticed by their old lusts and inhibited by their old fears. They rationalized their behavior by saying, "I know I shouldn't but I'd sure like to." Or, "I know I should but I'm afraid."

We are soldiers of Christ, the King of Kings before whom every knee on earth and under the earth and in the heavens will bow. Instead of acting like we're on the losing side, we should be saying, "I don't want to sin but I'm being attacked with urges. Now how can I fight back and who can help me?"

If we say, "I want to but I shouldn't..." then God and our friends can seem like "wet blankets." In our eyes, they are spoiling our happiness. We quickly and cleverly find a way around their objections and wise advice. However, if we say, "I don't want to but I'm being attacked," then God and our friends become our allies. We need each other in this effort.

Sometimes people come into my office and say "I can't understand what happened. I was doing really well and everything was going fine. Then all of a sudden I lost my temper and started yelling and screaming. The next thing I knew, I was right back into my old stuff...."

If I were to ask this person's friends and family, they would probably tell me that for hours, perhaps even for days before this outburst of anger occurred, they could see it coming. The man or woman who thought "I was doing really well," really wasn't doing well at all. In a state of self-delusion people often say, "No, no. I'm doing fine. I'm going to be OK. I promise—I'll be strong."

We need to have the support and encouragement of people whom we trust who can help us in the struggle. If we're humble enough to let them know what to watch for in the way of warning signals, our friends and family will be able to gently point them out to us whenever necessary. They can help us to watch for trouble.

I would suggest giving friends a written list of questions to ask us on a regular basis or whenever they become suspicious of our spiritual condition. Those questions will guarantee accountability. And knowing that our friends will be asking the questions will provide us with a strong motivation to resist sin.

Don't provide vague questions, like "How did you do this week?" Rather use very practical and specific questions such as "Did you raise your voice against your wife at all this week?" "Have you had any alcoholic drinks this week?" "Have you been eating properly this week?" "Were you able to avoid sexual lust this week?"

Keep in mind, however, that we aren't supposed to make it someone else's job to rescue us or keep us out of mischief or always be on the watch for us. Friends provide nothing more than extra help. We are the ones on the front lines watching for warning signals around us as well as in our own lives. When we sense danger in the air, we need to learn how to calm down and reorient ourselves.

HOW DO WE LOOSEN THE ENEMY'S GRIP?

Step number six: when trouble arises, reach out for help. We've already talked about lifting our eyes from the stormy waves and fixing them on Jesus. We do this by crying out "Help" and "Thanks," as well as by focusing on higher truths. But another vital strategy of warfare is to call out for help from those who understand our struggles.

In working with a lot of people who are involved with Alcoholics Anonymous, I've found that this organization works better than some of the other anonymous groups, even though they all use very similar ideas. In trying to figure out why, it has occurred to me that one of the reasons is that the AA sponsorship system is so well developed and managed. Experienced sponsors make themselves available to new people who need to learn the same kinds of lessons.

Do you have a safe person in your life whom you can call in times of trouble? If you don't, it's important for you to find someone. This person should agree to help you watch for trouble and be willing to receive your call for help whenever and however it may come. Ask God to show you whom you could trust for this important responsibility. Of course, once that connection is made, it is up to you to do the reaching out.

Sometimes we feel embarrassed about our struggles. That is why it is so important to remember that the signals of our weakness are not sin; they simply lead to sin. We need to thank God for those signals and stop feeling ashamed because of them. If we feel embarrassed because we have a lustful thought and choose not to admit its existence, we are quite likely to go ahead and indulge in lustful actions. But if we humbly call out to a friend when we're attacked by undesirable thoughts, we can receive the necessary support to avoid falling into that sinful behavior pattern.

Be aware that Satan loves to paralyze believers, to isolate them from others, to divide and conquer. I find it especially helpful here to focus on the positive task of rebuilding the walls rather than constantly ruminating on the rubble which proves my brokenness.

Support and help is what the body of Christ is all about. When (not if) we do blow it, hit the slippery hill, or fall into the pit, our Christian friends will help us get back up and reaffirm grace. And God will make something good out of our failure even though we will suffer some inevitable consquences. Our job is to help others help us. The devil lies and says, "If they really cared they'd just know what you need. Besides, you shouldn't ask—that would spoil everything." Don't listen to this lie.

When we share painful facts and feelings with our friends, they will volunteer to help. They want to meet our need. Yet when they suggest something we stomp all over their valuable opinions by saying, "Yes, but..." We may need Christian brothers and sisters to advise or to confront us. But we may need to say, "What I really need from you is for you to listen and help bear my burden, to pray for, to comfort, to encourage, to relate to me... have you ever been through something similar?"

You may find it helpful to share with them in four distinct areas:

1. My sinful reaction to the painful situation is _____
   and causes me to hurt God and others by _____.

2. My understanding of God's ideal reaction is _____.

3. Practically, what I've tried and plan to try is _____.

4. I realize I'm already valuable, that the power to change comes from God, and that I have hope. But I'd be grateful for your feedback.

Step number seven: loosen the enemy's hold by recalling past battles. First be clear about the behavior pattern you are trying to defeat. Renounce past involvements and declare that you belong to God. We are commanded in Leviticus 26:40 to confess our iniquities and the iniquities of our fathers. We need to recall our own sinful ways and those of our parents, no matter what it may have involved or how we feel about it. At that point we should declare, "I renounce the devil and all his ways." Especially renounce any personal or family dabbling in the occult.

One important issue which needs to be faced is our enjoyment of sin. To be strong in warfare, we must learn to hate even the relief and pleasure of sin. When the heat is on, we don't need some little inner voice saying, "But it felt so good," or "I can't let it go completely! There may be times I'll need that sin if my stress becomes too great or if God doesn't come through for me."

This unusually vicious terrorist incident illustrates sin's dangerous appeal. An aircraft flew low over a village located in the heart of a war zone. The poverty-stricken civilians who lived there were struggling to survive. They and their children had lost loved ones, done without food, and lived with constant fear for years. All at once, from the belly of the airplane, fell the most delightful dolls anyone in the village had ever seen. They were beautifully handcrafted, with lovely faces and exquisite clothes.

What a dream come true for those poor little children! They hadn't had playthings for as long as they could remember. They gathered up the inviting dolls and clustered around them, giggling, chattering, and admiring the dolls' smiling faces.

Then, without warning, one of the dolls exploded, killing several children and maiming others. Screaming and desperate, the boys and girls scattered. But across the village, the same scene was acted out. The admiration of the dolls. The abrupt explosion. The bloodied children. It happened again and again before the panic-striken adults could warn all the boys and girls.

The dolls actually served as time bombs delivered by an enemy aircraft. And it was their beauty that drew the children to embrace the hidden explosives.

How very like sin—lovely on the outside, meeting a need for diversion, arriving from out of the blue like a miraculous gift. But after embracing sin we discover death, destruction, and devastation. We need to despise sin's beauty and pleasure as well as its evil results, its enticements as well as its consequences.

Step number eight: confess to God, yourself, and others whatever you may have done in the past. In order to further loosen the enemy's grip, prepare a "how it was" list for yourself. On this list, ask the Holy Spirit to remind you of events in which you reacted by doing something sinful. Start with recent circumstances and work backward. Write down the triggers and excuses for the sin. Detail the excitement, relief, and long-term pain your wrongdoing produced. How did it affect your family? Your friends? God? Your own peace of mind?

Consider not only the wrong you did but also the hurt caused by what you *didn't* do while preoccupied with sin. What happened while you may have been wallowing in self-hatred, making excuses, and trying to pay for your failures? Make painful apologies and amends, and then steer clear of any paths that might lead you back to the sin.

HOW DO WE PLOT OUR FORWARD ADVANCEMENT?

The course of our lives is always changed by sin—that is one of its most predictable consequences. And no matter how we try, we can't force things back into place once sin has dislodged them. Suppose we're going along on path A. We sin, then get back up and say, "Sorry about that, Lord. I'll get back on path A."

God informs us, "No, path A isn't available to you anymore. But I've got a great path B for you."

We argue, "No, Lord, I want to go back to path A." We vehemently refuse to submit and try to get back on path A again. Before long we see that our effort to do so has turned out to be another sin. We repent of that and go to the Lord once again, "Sorry, Lord. I'll be glad to try path B."

God shakes his head and says "Well, path B is gone now but I have a great path C for you." Somewhere along the line we have to stop being stubborn and accept whatever the Lord has for us with gratitude rather than with arguments.

Most of all, our aim should be to avoid further sin. Besides altering our path or at least forcing us to take the long way around, sin hurts our relationship with God. How good to know that our relationship with our heavenly Father can be mended. Once we have dealt with past sin, confessed it, and given it to God, we have a new beginning. We've won back lost territory. We've re-established a fortified postion. And although the battle with temptation still rages, God has made it possible for us to hold the ground we've regained by learning new behaviors.

Step number nine: hold the ground you've regained, then move in the *opposite* direction of your past sin pattern. We often scratch our heads and wonder, "What's going on here? What is God trying to do in my life? What does he want to change?"

Sometimes we can find the answers we need by asking another very significant question: "What would Jesus do?" Having a clear picture in our minds of the life of Christ proves to be an invaluable guide for spiritual warfare. Jesus was tempted in every way we are tempted, but he never sinned. By studying the Gospels to explore Jesus' behavior, personality, and character, we can gain some idea of how he responded to various circumstances.

We may discover that Christ reacted to things far differently than we might have expected. We sometimes imagine that being like Jesus simply means keeping quiet and always being nice to everyone. But that's not true. Being like Jesus sometimes means speaking the truth very firmly. Sometimes it means taking a huge risk. Sometimes it requires reaching out healing hands with faith and spiritual power. There's really only one thing we can know for sure: being like Jesus always means dying to ourselves and to our old, ingrained ways of life.

Once we grasp something that God is saying to us, once we understand a principle he wants us to apply to our lives, it is up to us to obey. And obedience means moving the specific parts of our bodies according to God's principles whether we feel like it or not. This is faith in action. It means trying to move ahead in the indicated direction, not just for appearance's sake, but with a whole heart.

Many couples come to me who have already decided to get a divorce. Once that decision has been made, they make an appointment to see a "Christian shrink" who won't be able to help them. But they want to say "We've tried everything—even counseling—but we're just so incompatible; it's hopeless so we figure it's OK for us to move on." When I detect that kind of attitude, it saddens me. There's no point even in beginning. They've already planned the outcome; they're just trying to *look* good.

When we sincerely try, we cannot guarantee the results. The outcome of our effort is God's business. But when we honestly try to obey his Word, we can expect him to reward us, one way or another. If we simply look back and say, "I've learned my lesson," we haven't gone far enough. It is not enough to just try to quit our problems. We are supposed to move in a forward direction, away from sin toward righteousness. "For just as you have presented your members as servants to uncleanness, and to lawlessness leading to more lawlessness, even so now present your members as servants to righteousness for holiness" (Rom 6:19).

In his letter to the Ephesians, Paul rephrases this principle of moving in the opposite direction of our past sin in terms of the old nature and the new nature:

> But... you... have been taught by Him, as the truth is in Jesus: that you put off, concerning your former conduct, the old man which is corrupt according to the deceitful lusts, and be renewed in the spirit of your mind, and that you put on the new man which was created according to God, in righteousness and true holiness. Therefore, putting away lying, each one speak truth with his neighbor, for we are members of one another. "Be angry and do not sin": do not let the sun go down on your wrath, nor give place to the devil. Eph 4:20-27

I believe that the way that we put off the old nature and put on the new nature is not by making a continuous effort to be strong. It is rather by stating each day and each hour, "Lord, I can't, not in my strength. But I have you. So teach me to do the opposite of what my old nature dictates. Remind me that I'm already dead to sin and alive to you."

THE PRINCIPLE OF EQUAL AND OPPOSITE

This principle of moving in the equal and opposite direction of our sinful behavioral patterns can provide powerful clues to the question of how to advance in warfare. Let's examine a few specific examples to help you get a better feel for using this principle tool in your own struggle against sin.

Take anger, for example, which the Ephesians verse on the previous page mentions. Our uncontrolled anger can affect everyone we encounter. The wrath of human beings "does not produce the righteousness of God." What is its opposite? People usually answer "peace or joy or calmness." But I believe the opposite of anger is to be *angry without sinning*. Anger in itself is a good and useful emotion. Its pure expression reflects the fear of the Lord and hatred of evil. We need to react negatively to sin but in our anger we must not sin.

"Not letting the sun go down on our wrath" means dealing with it. Address the problems that caused the anger to begin with. Don't let it go on and on, festering and boiling into resentment. Don't give any room to the devil for mischief.

Another destructive behavioral pattern revolves around the words which come out of our mouths. Paul goes on to counsel the Ephesians, "Let no corrupt communication proceed out of your mouth, but what is good for necessary edification, that it may impart grace to the hearers" (Eph 4:29).

Do we attack grace in others? Do we call them worthless? Do we tell them, in so many words, that they are powerless and helpless and hopeless? If so, let us determine to begin walking down another path. We must remember the grace of others, remind them of grace, and minister grace to them.

Let us take to heart Paul's admonition of the Ephesians: "And do not grieve the Holy Spirit of God, by whom you were sealed for the day of redemption. Let all bitterness, wrath, anger, clamor, and evil speaking be put away from you, with all malice. And be kind to one another, tender hearted, forgiving one another, just as God in Christ also has forgiven you" (Eph 4:30-32).

What is the opposite of stealing? What would you recommend to a woman who came to you and said, "I've had a problem with stealing and I want to quit"? You would probably tell her to line up some avenue of accountability. That would be useful. You might also tell her to get a job if she doesn't already have one. Certainly that would be a good idea.

An even more specific suggestion would be to get a job working with the same parts of her body she used for stealing—a job using her hands. But that still wouldn't be enough. You could also recommend that she pay back whatever she had stolen, perhaps even two-fold or four-fold. Paying such a stiff penalty would strongly motivate a person to quit stealing.

But that still isn't the opposite. What is the opposite of taking? It is *giving*. That answer captures the essence of another verse of Scripture: "Let him who stole steal no longer, but rather let him labor, working with his hands and what is good, that he may have something to give him who has need" (Eph 4:28).

What is the opposite of perfectionism? The answer I usually hear is "sloppiness, carelessness, or not doing things thoroughly." Actually nothing could be farther from the truth. Most perfectionists swing on a pendulum between trying to do things too perfectly and giving up completely. Perfectionists are hardly perfect.

Perfectionism is the sin of trying to earn my grace, my sense of worth, strength, and security by doing tasks "perfectly." But who's to be the judge? The perfectionist is, of course, which means that nothing ever seems good enough. Some perfectionists do excellent work but derive no satisfaction from it. Some perfectionists give up completely and end up doing almost nothing. Deep inside they're still judging themselves by saying "I should be able to but I can't." Some of the worst workers I've ever encountered have been trapped in perfectionism.

One antidote to perfectionism is to do a lot of things well enough to make a positive contribution rather than doing one or two things flawlessly. The opposite of perfectionism is still excellence—but for the right reason. Once we have accepted our own value, we have nothing to prove, nothing to defend. We can therefore do things with excellence out of gratitude to the Lord. The final product may not change radically, but our motivation will be entirely different and much more pleasing to God. When we know that our worth comes from God, then he can delight with us in our efforts despite their inevitable flaws.

What is the opposite of workaholism? The opposite of being a workaholic doesn't mean being homeless, riding the rails, or living in a tent in the woods. In fact, I find that people who approach work from the right perspective usually accomplish much more than any workaholic ever could. Researchers have done studies to demonstrate that when a person comes to work on time, goes home at a reasonable time, and knows that the day can't be stretched endlessly, he or she actually gets more done than a workaholic.

Like perfectionists, workaholics use their work in an attempt to earn their value, as well as to avoid other responsibilities. Such a skewed perspective tends to produce inefficiency since that kind of person unconsciously approaches the work day as endless. The opposite of workaholism is not to accomplish less, but to work for the sake of serving God and others. We get up in the morning at a reasonable time, work with joy, quit when it is time to quit and sleep soundly (see Psalm 127).

What is the opposite of alcoholism? Obviously, an alcoholic can't turn over a new leaf by drinking with a new purpose or attitude. A person addicted to alcohol needs to renounce the offending substance completely. And alcoholism is not just a matter of drinking alcohol. It involves an unhealthy approach to all of life, one which affects spirit, mind, will, emotion, body, and community.

Studying individual behavior patterns can provide helpful clues for truly embarking on a new path to holiness. For example, those who have started fights can seek to become peace-makers. Male alcoholics who have tended to be out of the house frequently can become deeply involved with the family. Those who have eroded their family's spirituality could choose to initiate both personal and family devotions. Those who have skipped work ought to become reliable. Those who have avoided church need to begin to participate more actively.

Addiction to alcohol abuses the body; alcoholics should learn to care for their bodies by eating and exercising properly. Since alcoholics drink to drown their emotional pain, they must learn to bear discomfort and not run from it, if long-lasting and deep-down change is ever to take place. Many people who go to AA and quit drinking never grasp the fact that they need a new mind, a new heart, and a new will.

No matter what your weaknesses may be, no matter how you act out your bitterness, drivenness, or escapism, seeking to do the equal and opposite behavior will transform your life; it will renew your mind.

OVERCOMING ADDICTIONS AND SINFUL BEHAVIORAL PATTERNS

As we have already seen, addictions arise as ways to escape the painful reality of our weakness and the equal pain of being stuck in bitterness. We find some way to feel better while running from responsibility and our desperate need for grace.

What is the opposite of this kind of thinking? Overcoming addictions means accepting our humble position under grace and diving into the work and the warfare. We rejoice in the privilege of being fellow laborers in rebuilding the walls, fellow sufferers with Christ. When discomfort is an integral part of our obedience, then we count it as a privilege.

As we surrender an addiction we suffer the pain of seeing the truth about ourselves, of having others see the truth about us, of withdrawing from the substance physically and emotionally, of facing the tasks which we used to escape. These discomforts must be counted "all joy" (Jas 1:2). Don't tally up your discomforts because those who do so soon come to believe they've earned the right to relapse into sin.

How about reversing sinful behavioral patterns? In chapter eight, I asked you to determine which pattern in your life you would especially like to change. Is it something small or a major obstacle? What would be the opposite behavior? If you're not sure, risk a heart-to-heart talk with some of your friends. Ask them if they have any idea what the opposite of that behavior might be. Ask them if they'll walk through the process of examining it with you. You'll definitely need support in reversing your tracks—never an easy proposition for creatures of habit.

Be prepared not to perform perfectly. Sometimes you will forget completely to stop and do the opposite. But as you continue your efforts by the grace of God, you can put into practice these simple tools in reversing the sinful behavioral patterns in your own life. When you are tripped up:

- Catch yourself
- Pause
- Calm down
- Assess the situation
- Determine what God wants you to do
- Gather your resources
- Obey in a way opposite to your habitual sin pattern
- Rest
- Get ready for the next time

Perhaps the most important thing of all is to remember that when you get knocked down, with God's help you can get right back up again. Little by little you'll find yourself growing, changing, and getting stronger.

BEATING THE DEVIL AT HIS GAME

You can be guaranteed of one fact: our struggle for holiness will not go uncontested. Consider the devil's tactic of enticing us to sin and then beating up on us afterward. What does the devil whisper in your ear when you've been doing well for a while and a temptation crosses your path? What are some of the thoughts he plants in your head? "Well, go ahead. You've earned it." Or, "Who's going to know?" Or, "It's just a little indulgence, after all, and compared with all the good things you've done, what does it really matter in the long run?"

The devil is not above reminding us of the grace of God when it serves his own purposes. "Well, if you sin God will pour out his grace and make something good come of it. He's not going to be angry at you and judge you. Go ahead and sin and let grace abound—you'll have better stories to tell."

Suppose we listen to the devil and indulge in the sin. Doesn't he kind of change his tune at that point? Does the devil put his arm around us and comfort us by saying "No big deal"? Not a chance. He'll clobber you and shout, "You worthless scum! You hopeless wretch! There is absolutely no help for you anymore."

The devil will even quote Scripture to prove his point: "Having put your hand to the plow and turned back, you are now unfit for the kingdom of heaven." He'll keep driving us down into the ground until we agree, "Since I've already blown it I might as well go ahead and sin some more." That spells a momentary victory—for the wrong side.

I remember one woman who had been trying to discipline herself in the area of weight. She had done really well for a week, but meanwhile felt she really should continue to bake and cook special goodies for her family. One day she walked into the kitchen and noticed a piece missing out of the chocolate cake she had just baked. No one else was in the house. No one else could have eaten it. Without realizing she had done it, this woman had eaten a piece of the cake! Feeling devastated, she said to herself, "Oh, this is terrible. What if someone finds out? What am I going to do with the evidence?" She proceeded to eat the rest of the cake and then bake a new one.

Satan loves to get us into that kind of behavior. But God's approach to facing temptation is far different. The Lord reminds us, "Don't do it. Rely on me. I will give you the power. I will give you the way out. Remember, if you sin there will be consequences." Then, if we choose to sin anyway, the Lord comes to us and reassures us, "Get up. I can make something good out of this, too. It won't be quite the way it could have been, but it will be good."

Our best bet is to avoid the slippery hill. But when we do skid and hit the bottom, it's really important to get right up immediately. Watch out for the depressing thought, "If only I'd learned years ago." Yes, that would have been better. But negative ideas like that will only drive us deeper into despair and sin. Life is not about arriving at a goal. Life is a continual journey.

Are you doing better? Thank the Lord. But that certainly doesn't mean that you have arrived. You still have those same weaknesses lurking somewhere in the shadows. Always remember it was God's strength, and his strength alone, that got you through this far. And it is the grace of God that will carry you on.

Generational sins. Here's a sobering truth for parents to ponder: they are influencing their children with everything they do. We read many examples of this principle in the Bible. Abraham, Isaac, Jacob, and their descendants shared a propensity for lying, deceiving, and cheating. This pattern of sin was passed from one generation to the next. You are the product of your parents, and your children will repeat your patterns of behavior.

This awareness can motivate you when you're tired and struggling. "Wait a minute. It's worth it. This problem goes all the way back to my great-grandfather. But if I'm willing to fight, I won't pass it on to my kids."

Struggling against sin in your own life—even if you don't feel like you're making much progress—is well worth the blood, sweat, and tears. Your obedience releases God's power into the situation and gives him glory. Your children will not have as much trouble with the basic family weaknesses as you are having.

When we want to protect the body from bacterial invasion, what do we do? We inject an attenuated form of the bacteria which the body learns to detect and resist. In the same way our children see our struggles and learn to fight the problem. Even the struggle itself inoculates your family against the lies of the evil one. They see what happens to you and they say "Boy, I don't want to get into that." But if we yield to sin, our children may decide to practice to the extreme what we tolerate in moderation.

PUTTING HUMPTY DUMPTY TOGETHER AGAIN

Step number ten: heal the whole person by rebuilding your life better than ever. Once we have made some positive progress, we want to feel that our lives are having a positive effect on others. We are not only valuable because God loves us, although that surely encourages us. We are not only valuable because we are well designed, although that, too, serves as an encouragement. *We also need to know that we are needed.*

One of the most difficult groups of people to reach are those who have been very active in the church but who now have lost their ability to perform in the same ways. They can easily become bitter at themselves, at God, and at the church itself. Even if they know their value isn't *increased* by service, they can still feel it is *decreased* when they can't serve.

As Paul points out in 1 Corinthians 12, a properly run church fully embraces the people we think we need the least (or who feel they are the least). In fact, these people prove to be the most necessary and we should thus grant them the greatest honor and protection. We should uplift them with our prayers and our encouragement. And most important, we ought to discover how we need them and draw them into ministry.

What about you? Do you sometimes feel like you are the least valuable or the weakest? Are you willing to reach out to find out where you are needed? So often we don't like to take the risk of reaching out and doing what little we can. Maybe at one time you could have done a great deal more. Or perhaps you long to do what someone else can. It's time you carefully consider your own design and decide that you're going to like being you.

As a young lad I knew one woman who, as she grew elderly, had more and more difficulty seeing her value. Having no family of her own, she had been consigned to a nursing home. At this point in her life, this woman had decided life wasn't worth living and was praying that God would take her home. She sincerely wanted to die.

But a godly family on a farm near the nursing home decided that they weren't going to let her go that easily. They valued this woman. The parents lived with several teenagers in a huge, rambling farmhouse. One afternoon they drove over to the convalescent home, picked up the old woman, and brought her to their house. She wasn't a relative of theirs but they had gotten permission from her guardians.

Before long, they had checked her out of the hospital and she was living with the family. This elderly woman became a beloved grandmother-figure to those teenagers and a source of spiritual encouragement to everyone in the family. She couldn't hear very well and had to get around in a wheelchair, but the family provided her with a desk in front of a big picture window over-looking the farm. As far as anyone could tell, she proceeded to correspond with every missionary in the world. In fact, when I went to visit her, she smiled, reached into her desk, and pulled out a letter from my brother who is a missionary in Brazil.

Sometimes we slip out the back door by saying, "All I can do is pray." If all you can really do is pray, prayer is more than enough. Perhaps when you pray, you feel as if you're saying some not-too-eloquent words. But the Holy Spirit can breathe life and power into them. He receives your feeble prayers and translates them into God's language. He will pray for you and through you.

Besides praying—which we are all called upon to do—you may be able to make some other important contributions. You can write letters to people in jail or on the mission field. You can encourage your friends by telephone. You can bake cookies for the church school. You can send birthday cards, anniversary cards, or notes of encouragement. You can visit the elderly in convalescent hospitals. You can host Bible studies in your home. And those are just the obvious possibilities. Ask God to show you what you, and maybe you alone, can do to influence the world around you.

You need to be needed, so take the risk. You may have to be a little feisty about it. One day when Jesus was ministering, a Phoenician woman came up to him with a deep concern for her daughter (see Mt 15:21-28). In fact, her concern was so great that she wasn't going to give up, no matter what.

This impassioned mother came to Jesus and said, "Son of David, have mercy on me and my daughter." He ignored her until the disciples were frustrated and asked him to deal with her.

He replied to them, "It is not right to take food from the

children and give it to the dogs."

What?! But the Lord knew what he was doing. He was testing the woman's resolve. She worshiped and said, "Sir, the puppies get to eat the crumbs that fall from the children's table."

What humility! God honored this mother's tenacity. Jesus gave her the desire of her heart and her daughter was healed. The woman's daughter needed her and the devoted mother found a way of helping her daughter. She wouldn't take no for an answer when she saw that Jesus had left a crack in the door for someone bold enough to push it open.

Your willingness to keep up the fight for spiritual blessing will be rewarded. Your desire to help others will help win the battle. This kind of heart in action indicates that you are looking beyond merely overcoming negative patterns of behavior. Your victory involves not only quitting the old ways, but developing good attitudes like gratitude, fear of the Lord, and enthusiasm in the midst of the struggle.

Maintaining the temple of God. Besides healing your mind, will, spirit, and emotions, God wants to heal your body, too. What are some of the components of the body that can be refined, developed, and disciplined? How can the human body become a delight to God and a powerful tool in his hands?

What we call "the flesh" includes physical strength, alertness, coordination, and the five senses. These are elements that we can develop. When our inner lives are brought into God's peace, our physical bodies are able to respond positively. Our pulse rate can stabilize. Our blood pressure can become lower. Our stress-related headaches, backaches, and stomach problems can diminish. Our psychosomatic illnesses can be much relieved.

If we are to provide good maintenance for our bodies—which are the temple of God (1 Cor 6:19)—we have to think about eating properly, getting appropriate exercise and rest, and not abusing ourselves. Our bodies are precious to God and his special gift to us. We are not supposed to sin against them, either through carnal activities or through negligence. If we die ten years early because we have not cared for ourselves properly, we are doing a grave disservice to the greater body—the body of Christ, his church.

Taking time to enjoy life. It is a wonderfully healthy thing simply to delight in life. But some people feel it is a sin to enjoy things. Even the Lord himself was criticized by the Pharisees when he took pleasure in food, drink, and friendship: "See? He likes being with those people. He is a wine lover and a glutton!" The Pharisees thought nobody should enjoy anything, and sad to say, we still have a few of those types of people around in our churches today.

I think that we do our Creator a grave disservice not to enjoy the wonderful things that have come from his hand. If God had wanted to, he could have designed a huge, flat, and monotonous planet. He could have planted only one kind of bush, covered with very nutritious but boring berries. Those berries might not taste very good, but they would meet all our needs.

But God didn't do that. He is a God who delights in variety. And in his creative exuberance he designed an almost infinite assortment of plants, animals, minerals, mountains, oceans, clouds, stars, and human beings. He composed an endless symphony of sounds. He filled the world with light and fragrance and ever-changing colors. We aren't supposed to worship his creations, but to worship the Creator who gave them to us. When we give a gift, our greatest recompense is to watch the recipient's delight in the gift. Why not worship God by "considering the lilies"?

Humility before the Creator enables us to give up our prideful, self-centered point of view. It shows us the way to a new way of life. The One who made us is drawing us away from self-trust, self-reliance, and self-power. He is calling us to faith—faith in who he is, in what he wants to accomplish, and in what he is able to do, faith that leads us to a new way of living.

CHAPTER

10 | In Case of Emergency...

WHILE READING a Christian magazine some time ago, I came across an article which had been written by a woman suffering from periodic depression. This woman explained that for a few months she would do fairly well emotionally. Then, for as long as three months at a time, she would encounter heavy, dark depression. She had tried medication; she had tried counsel; she had certainly tried prayer. In her case God had simply said, "My grace is sufficient for you." God sovereignly chose not to heal the woman's depression, at least for the time being.

Now we know that depression itself is not sin, but that it can easily provoke sinful responses. When this Christian woman felt well she would use the time to prepare for those inevitable months ahead when she knew she would plunge into the darkness of the valley. She was determined to glorify God no matter how she felt.

To help this woman of faith accomplish her goal, she kept a shoe box handy in which she collected poems, articles, hymns, verses, and other items of encouragement which brought her some measure of relief. On top of the box she taped a check list. Whenever she became depressed she mechanically went through her list and found comfort. She called this box of encouragement her "Emergency Kit."

Does God's Word anywhere outline the possible contents of an emergency kit which would provide comfort? Philippians 4 says, "Be anxious for nothing, but..." And in the words that follow, we find some extremely useful responses for difficult times.

When problems overwhelm us and provoke anxiety, what do we usually do? We already feel bad enough about the circumstances, and then our unhappiness just makes matters worse. We often take responsibility for things that are none of our business rather than giving them to God. We look at the problem and conclude that nothing good can come from it.

After we have chased ourselves well down the path of worry, we collect all the negative details we can get our hands on and obsessively run them round and round in our minds. Then we look at the problem and refuse to do anything about it. We sort of give up, assuming that the little we could do wouldn't make any difference anyway.

This chasing round and round after our tails often stems from our human tendency to focus on our own needs. Like an old spiritual we begin to moan, "Nobody knows the trouble I've seen...." And then we top it all off by worrying about what other people will think.

Paul recommends the exact opposite response in his letter to the Philippians. By now, that shouldn't surprise us. Doing the opposite of our usual human response is a basic scriptural principle.

Be anxious for nothing, but in everything by prayer and supplication, with thanksgiving, let your requests be made known to God; and the peace of God, which surpasses all understanding, will guard your hearts and minds through Christ Jesus. Finally, brethren, whatever things are true, whatever things are noble, whatever things are just, whatever things are pure, whatever things are lovely, whatever things are of good report, if there is anything praiseworthy—meditate on these things. **Phil 4:6-8**

MAKING YOUR OWN EMERGENCY KIT

With these verses from Philippians as our guide, how would you go about making an emergency kit for yourself? I will suggest quite a few different items for inclusion, but you should adapt the kit according to your own particular struggles and circumstances.

How can you learn to respond to emotional emergencies? The first three steps you should always take in an emotional emergency are easy to memorize as you go about your daily life. Once you've learned these automatic responses, put them to work every time you are attacked, every time you feel irritated, every time you feel depressed.

1. *Help!*
   - I can't handle this situation, because I can do nothing without you, Lord. You be my strength.
   - I can't handle my reaction to this situation. You be my peace. Teach me to rest and wait on you.
   - Help me to reach out and receive help from my brothers and sisters in Christ.
   - Help me to hate only sin, and not to be anxious about discomfort or dysfunction.
   - Help me to cling to the unchangeable truths that I tend to forget.
   - Help me to remember those truths and not to resist you when you hold me to them.

2. *Thank you, Lord.*
   - Thank you that you intend good to come from this problem, even though others may intend it for evil.
   - Thank you for working in me, doing whatever you want for your pleasure.

3. *What is your will?*
   - You have promised to give wisdom to me if I ask for it (Jas 1:5-8).
   - You have committed yourself to guide me and to

walk with me even through the valley of the shadow of death.

- You have a plan in this situation and I ask you to reveal it to me. I will not be double-minded once I have received your wisdom.

Start by placing these three simple responses in your emergency kit: "Help"; "Thank you, Lord"; and "What is your will?" Carry them around in your head and practice them. Every time something unpleasant happens—traffic lights are too long, people aren't driving right, weather is bad, someone criticizes you, whatever—start at the top of the list.

You might want to sum up the details of these three responses by writing some variation of what I call "crisis prayers."

Crisis prayer number one: *Lord, I'm going to need your help in dealing with this issue. The outcome is yours and I can only try. I even need your help in getting my emotions under control because I realize I usually overreact.*

Crisis prayer number two: *Lord, I thank you for this problem. Thanks for what you are going to do through it to help me grow, benefit others, and bring yourself glory.*

Crisis prayer number three: *Lord, show me your will as I seek to focus on you. Help me to want what you want. Work in me to will and to do according to your good pleasure.*

Some people type their emergency kit information on three-by-five cards and carry them in a pocket or purse. Others record these messages on a cassette. Instead of trying to concentrate on reading when they're under attack, they play the tape back to themselves. Actually hearing the truth can work powerfully to erase all those destructive mental tapes we tend to play over and over.

SPELLING OUT OUR THANKS

We should be most grateful to God for who he is and what he has done to restore us to himself. Giving thanks means recognizing the bottom line: our life is in God alone. The following prayers could also prove helpful in your emergency kit. Relief may be spelled R-O-L-A-I-D-S in television commercials, but I find the longest lasting relief in case of spiritual indigestion comes from a strong dose of T-R-U-T-H.

> *Thank you, Lord, because no matter what the outcome of this particular battle, in you I am: dead to sin; alive to God; immortal; beloved; victorious; stronger than he that is in the world; clean; righteous; sanctified; Abba's child; saved; equipped with truth; seated in heaven; and mighty for warfare.*

> *Thank you, Lord. The results are yours, but you will always use my efforts: to bring glory to yourself; to benefit others; to develop in me the character of Christ; to store up treasure in heaven for me; to increase my fellowship with you and my enjoyment of you; to bring pleasure to you; and to bring me inner peace.*

Another helpful tool in spelling out our thanks to the Lord involves calling to mind his many Hebrew names. God's absolute holiness prohibited the Jewish people from calling God by name, so they used many endearments to reflect the precious aspects of his character. The God of Abraham, Isaac, and Jacob is also our God. Praying in the following way can release streams of grace to refresh your mind and spirit: *You are my God, and you have been working in my life...*

- *to provide for my basic needs: you are* El Shaddai, *the All-Sufficient One, the "breast."*
- *to help me worship; you are* El Elyon, *the Most High.*
- *to create in me new thoughts, new feelings, and a new will; you are* Elohim, *the Creator.*
- *to give me purpose and vision, something for which to fight; you are* Jehovah Nissi, *"The Lord is my banner."*
- *to give me atonement and cleansing; you are* Jehovah Hereh, *"the Lord who provides a sacrifice."*
- *to give me a sense of unexplainable peace; you are* Jehovah Shalom, *"the Lord is my peace."*
- *to give me strength; you are* Jehovah Saabaoth, *"the Lord of Hosts."*

- *to comfort me with your presence; you are* El Roi, *"the One who sees and cares even for sparrows, and* El Shamma, *"the God who is there."*
- *to help me feel special and set apart for you; you are* Jehovah Mekoddishkem, *"The Lord, my sanctification."*
- *to heal me; you are* Jehovah Rapha, *"the Lord, my Healer."*
- *to lead and guide me; you are* Jehovah Yaah, *"the Lord, my Shepherd."*
- *to convict me; you are* Quanna, *"Jealous for my heart."*
- *to give me perspective; you are* El Olam, *"the everlasting Lord who will be mine for all eternity."*
- *to remind me that I belong to you; you are* Adonai, *"the One who owns me."*
- *to remind me that your truth stands on its own; you are* Yahweh, *"the self-existent Truth."*
- *to remind me that I am already dead to sin and alive to you, to help me feel clean; you are* Jehovah Sidkeno, *"the Lord is my righteousness."*

Your emergency kit can also be stocked with a list of your own personal strengths and limitations, which was discussed in chapter one. This list can be headed by the prayer: *Thank you, Lord. I am myself, and I am fearfully and wonderfully made.*

Another helpful item is a page listing the exact thought-lies that trouble you followed by the truths which contradict them. For example, "I am worthless" can be countered by "I am bought with a great price"; "I am helpless" by "God is my refuge and strength"; or "I am hopeless" by "Christ in me is my hope." A prayer to accompany this page could be simply stated: *Thank you, Lord. Your truth overcomes lies.*

In Proverbs 10:24 we are warned that ungodly fears come true. The counteracting truth is: godly desires are granted. A list of fears/godly desires might include these kinds of statements, for example:

- Fear: "My wife might leave me."
- Godly desire: "I desire an intimate, unconditional, lasting relationship."

- Fear: "My children might rebel."
- Godly desire: "I desire godly children who allow me to guide and protect them."

Another helpful addition to your emergency kit is to make a collection of your favorite songs, poems, verses, letters, or whatever else God uses to comfort you. Read them or sing them over again when you feel the need for encouragement, thanking God for his inexhaustible reserves of comfort. After you have immersed yourself in God's love, take the opportunity to ask the Lord for guidance: *Guide me, Lord. I have been falling into the trap of deciding for myself what is right and what is wrong. What would you have me do?*

Some practical sources of guidance may be your personal life-savers. I have found tremendous help in the slender book entitled *In His Steps* by Charles Sheldon. Constantly listen for the still, small voice of God. Be aware of "coincidences." God is the God of coincidence; he arranges every little detail. Be sure to seek godly counsel from some Christian whom you trust. James 1:5-8 promises that God will give us wisdom if we ask for it in faith and single-minded trust. Read these verses and ask for wisdom. Expect it.

Once you have asked for guidance, you may have to wait for some answers. But meanwhile you may want to employ other principles and truths you already know about. For example, you could put together a "gratitude memory jogger." At noon list one thing God did for you in the morning; at supper list one thing God did in the afternoon; and at bedtime list one thing he did in the evening. As you begin to express your gratitude for little things, you'll begin to see God's action in all of life.

The following checklist may be a helpful tool for your emergency kit to remind you how much God has done for you. Read it over until you find an item for which to give him honor: "God has comforted, guided, convicted, encouraged, taught, reminded, empowered, protected, healed, provided for, arranged special timing of circumstances, worked out a ministry opportunity, etc." Now write, *Lord, you* _____
_____. *Thank you!*

We are designed to feel miserable when there seems to be nothing we can do about our problems. That's why prayer is so essential. We can always pray. Praying for enemies drives away bitterness, while praying for friends and loved ones drives away worry. Let us resolve to be obedient to God in this matter of prayer: *I will pray for those who love me and for those who don't. I will pray for those in authority, both in the world and in the church.*

You could write out a list of specific names and needs for which you could pray, whether you feel like it or not. For example, you could list any enemies or anyone who makes your life miserable. Alongside each name, list the particular need for which you want to pray. For example, you could pray for the salvation of your enemies or for a closer walk with God. Or you could ask God to reconcile you with your enemies and bring peace between you.

You might want to pray for specific people who struggle with problems much like your own. Ask God to help them to walk in God's truth. You could list political or religious leaders and ask God to give them truth, wisdom, and strength. You could list all the people you know with confidence that they all need health and hope and would appreciate your prayers. These kinds of prayers release God's grace, as well as help to get your mind off of yourself.

After you've obeyed the Lord and prayed to the Lord, you have done all you can do. It is time for you to simply rest in him, in his power, his provision, and his protection. *Lord, give me rest. Thank you for helping me try. My trying is valuable, no matter what the results. The results are yours, Lord. My worth, strength, and hope are in you and you alone. I refuse to fear anyone or anything but you. I know and believe that you love me.*

A QUICK REVIEW

A quick review of some of the truths that we have already covered in this book would help you in case of emergency. Many of my patients use the following questions and answers to help them to get refocused on God and his principles. Maybe they will encourage you as well.

Which part of any effort in obedience belongs to God? Whether God produces the following or not, it is not my job: to produce results; to generate motivation; to be worthy; to understand *why* (my job is to understand what God wants and *how* he wants to do it, but not *why*); to be strong; to pick the perfect time, place, or method.

What does it mean to "walk the second mile"? When someone tries to force me to do things that are irritating, although not sinful, I will: choose to do more than I'm asked; watch my attitude; let God teach me through the irritation.

What are the three steps of applied grace? Value myself because God does. Obey in confidence. Rest, leaving the results to God.

What questions should I ask myself before making a choice? What will people say about God after watching me? What needs can I meet for others by doing this? What character quality can I develop through this? How will this count in one hundred years? Will this push me closer to God? How will this make God feel? Will I have peace in my heart after my choice?

What is a personality disorder? It is a lifelong, habitual, and ineffective way of dealing with people and situations. To the person with the disorder, his way makes sense. However, in reality his way reflects an inability to be flexible and open to God and others.

How can I effectively react to an "ambush"? Having prepared myself for this in advance, I catch myself reacting to something. I calm down and take a deep breath. I talk to someone or refer to my emergency kit. I reorient myself to truth. I obey God's principles. I rest and leave the results to him.

What are the four points to consider regarding any issue or problem?

1. The power comes from God and he will help me. I'm already valuable and can't lose that. There is good reason to hope.
2. What about me needs to change?
3. What does God say on the subject?
4. What can a weak person like me do to cooperate with him?

What are the five parts of my identity? God-given strengths; God-given limitations; leftovers of past sin; unchangeable features (neither strengths nor weaknesses); and support systems (church, family, friends, books, other helps).

What is humility? In spite of recognizing and acknowledging all my weakness, blindness, instability, and poverty, humility is liking myself, because God does; being confident in his strength; and resting in God, because results are always his.

What is greed? Greed is being driven to obtain something in order to earn my worth, strength, and hope.

What is the opposite of greed? Building my hope in eternal values; fearing the Lord; and hating evil and loving good.

What is bitterness? Bitterness is earning my "godhood" by making myself the judge (Jas 4:11).

What is the opposite of bitterness? Acting in love for the welfare of others and having gratitude to God in all things.

What is sensuality or lust? Lust is preserving my "godhood" by creating a "god" which I think I can control. This god makes me feel valuable, strong, and secure when I consume it.

What is the opposite of sensuality or lust? Acting in faith by obeying God's principles and rejoicing in the struggle.

To what six things do we attach our sense of value? Accomplishments, approval, acceptance, possessions, power/control, and religiosity.

What are some conditions which we use as excuses to sin? Being bored, lonely, apathetic, tired, hungry, excited, rejected, enraged, depressed, and countless others!

What are the steps of an effective apology? God is convicting me of my wrong attitude of _____, which caused me to hurt you by _____. I know you must have felt _____ ___. I'd like to make amends by _____. I'm obtaining support and accountability from _____. I am not asking you to take a risk on a relationship with me because I deserve it. In fact if I were you I'd be nervous about taking such a risk. Maybe we could start by _____. If you'd forgive me now I'd be so grateful. (Be specific. Don't include the other person's part in the problem, don't make excuses; don't make promises to be strong.)

If I hate any human being, including myself, who else do I hate? GOD.

How should I respond to attacks upon my sense of value? I have no value of my own. But I am valuable because Jesus died for me, because God did a good job in designing me, and because God will act through me and bless my efforts. Therefore I like myself.

How should I respond to attacks upon my sense of hope and security? I cannot secure my future. But God has already done so. I am resting in him and in his good plans for me.

How should I respond to attacks upon my sense of strength? I am powerless. ("I can't.") But God can do anything through me. ("But God can.") So I'm obeying him in spite of my weakness. ("So here goes...")

What are some tools of hypocrisy which I use to tell myself, "I'm not so bad!"?
- Denial: "I have no problem."
- Vagueness: "I'm sure I have a problem somewhere."
- Minimization: "I guess, maybe, sort of, a little."
- Balance: trying to counteract bad by doing good.
- Blaming or excusing: "It's your fault."
- Comparisons: "I'm not as bad as he is."
- Abdication: "It's just the way I am."
- Agreement: "Yes, I'm a mess," then do nothing with the insight.

What are the stages of grief and/or repentance?
1. Denial/hypocrisy.
2. Reporter (facts without feelings).
3. Feelings of:
   a. anger
   b. sorrow
   c. helplessness, hopelessness, worthlessness.
4. Bargaining about the consequences.
5. Acceptance of reality; of God, self, and others.
6. Allowing God to bring forth healing and good.
7. Rejoicing in God. What others meant for evil, he meant for good.

How should I pray when I am bitter? Lord, help me to value you, the other person, and myself no matter what. Teach me the same lesson he (or she) needs to learn. Have mercy, he doesn't know what he's doing to me. Thank you for your mercy. Open his eyes by taking away peer support, by bringing discomfort, by taking away the pleasure of sin.

What does forgiveness mean and what doesn't it mean? Forgiveness does mean to let go of the offense. Don't use the details of the wrong to excuse further sin on your part. Be involved, but carefully. Prepare to minister to the other's needs. Set limits and walk through the consequences with the offender. Live abundantly and invite the offender to join in. Be prepared to take reasonable risks based on godly responsibility. Forgiveness *does not mean* forgetting, trusting, not setting consequences, pretending it never happened, fixing the other person.

When I am in the wrong and am being confronted, what should I do? Agree quickly, apologize, ask for mercy, and make amends (don't try to minimize the consequences or cover up).

What are the steps of an appeal? I like your good goal of _____. I see why your goal is so important to you because _____. I appreciate you for your efforts and character, for example _____. I have the same goal as you, and have helped accomplish it by _____. I'm concerned that your current method might not accomplish the good goal because _____ _____, I suggest _____. I'd be willing to help by _____. What do you think?

What does pride make me do? It makes me try to be my own god and reject grace by earning my own value, generating my own strength, and securing my own future. Pride makes me feel that if I'm to succeed, I must be perfect in all areas of my life forever. If I fail, pride makes me hate myself, blame someone else, deny/minimize my failure, or drown out my disappointment.

What are the three steps in a godly response to stress? Ask for God's help. Give God thanks. Ask God for guidance.

What are the three internal needs all people share? To belong. To be unique. To be needed.

What is grace? Grace is the free, undeserved gift from God to me which provides what I desperately need in order to deal with sin, yet could not generate for myself. Grace gives me:
- *Value:* cleansing, forgiveness, atonement, adoption, and sanctification, despite all past sin—mine or others'.

- *Power:* the will to not sin today because God is with me. (God will not "do it" for me or make me independently strong but he walks the valley beside me.)
- *Hope:* security not to sin tomorrow since God is there already, giving the same power he gave today.

The gift of grace cost God an infinite price. If I accept it, my reasonable response is to give him the only acceptable gift in return: myself. In giving myself to God, I am not merely a slave, but I am the Father's child.

SCRIPTURES TO INCLUDE IN YOUR EMERGENCY KIT

Help
James 1:5
Psalm 12:1
Psalm 22:10
Psalm 40: 1, 2, 3

Thanks
Romans 8:18
1 Peter 5:10
James 1:2-3
1 Peter 4:16
2 Corinthians 1:4-5

Who God Is
Jeremiah 9:23-24
Zephaniah 3:17
Philippians 1:6
1 Samuel 12:22
Psalm 23:3

My Identity
Isaiah 43:7
2 Corinthians 12:9-10
Psalm 139:13-16
1 Timothy 4:4-5

Romans 8:15
1 John 3:1

Reviewing God's Work
Philippians 2:13
Deuteronomy 6:7-8

Praying for Others
Hebrews 10:22
James 4:8
Matthew 5:44

My Thoughts and Words
Ephesians 5:19
Philippians 4:8

Positional Truth
John 1:12
Romans 2:7
John 3:16
Ephesians 3:17
Colossians 1:27
Romans 12:1-2
Philippians 1:20
1 Peter 2:24
Romans 6:10-11
Philippians 4:7
Ephesians 3:19
Romans 3:22
2 Corinthians 5:21
1 John 3:19
Romans 6:13

God's Rewards
Matthew 6:19-21
Matthew 5:16
Hebrews 11:6
Romans 8:29
Philippians 2:13

Other Books of Interest
by Servant Publications

Grace Works
Letting God Rescue You from Empty Religion
Dudley Hall

For those who are tired of struggling, feeling guilty, and never measuring up, the simple message of grace will breathe life back into them. *Grace Works* will show readers how to forgive themselves, relax in God's mercy, and enjoy his unconditional acceptance. Best of all, through grace God invites Christians to step out of religion into a passionate love relationship with him. When all else fails, God's grace really does work. *$9.99*

Forgiving Our Parents, Forgiving Ourselves
Healing Adult Children of Dysfunctional Families
Dr. David Stoop and Dr. James Masteller

Dr. Stoop explores the family patterns that perpetuate dysfunction. As we develop greater understanding of our family of origin, we will be able to take the essential step of forgiveness. We will find ourselves moving into a place of profound spiritual healing which will change our lives forever.
$10.99

Available at your Christian bookstore or from:
Servant Publications • Dept. 209 • P.O. Box 7455
Ann Arbor, Michigan 48107
Please include payment plus $1.25 per book
for postage and handling.
Send for our FREE catalog of Christian
books, music, and cassettes.

Other Books of Interest
from Servant Publications

Grace Works
Letting God Rescue You from Empty Religion
Dudley Hall

For those who are tired of struggling, feeling guilty, and never measuring up, the simple message of grace will breathe life back into them. *Grace Works* will show readers how to forgive themselves, relax in God's mercy, and enjoy his unconditional acceptance. Best of all, through grace God invites Christians to step out of religion into a passionate love relationship with him. When all else fails, God's grace really does work.

6 x 9 paper, **$10.99**

Forgiving Our Parents, Forgiving Ourselves
Healing Adult Children of Dysfunctional Families
Dr. David Stoop and Dr. James Masteller

Dr. Stoop explores the family patterns that perpetuate dysfunction. As we develop greater understanding of our family of origin, we will be able to take the essential step of forgiveness. We will find ourselves moving into a place of profound spiritual healing which will change our lives forever. *6 x 9 paper,* **$12.99**

Available at your Christian bookstore or from:
**Servant Publications • Dept. 209 • P.O. Box 7455
Ann Arbor, Michigan 48107**
Please include payment plus $1.25 per book
for postage and handling.
*Send for our FREE catalog of Christian
books, music, and cassettes.*